An Incorruptible Crown

PREVIOUSLY PUBLISHED
WITH RESOURCE PUBLICATIONS

Nonfiction

Storms Are Faith's Workout: Preparing Christians for Spiritual Ambush (2018).
Faith's Journey Confronts Obstacles: Instructing God's Soldiers to Overcome in His Armor (2019).
Satan's Strategy to Torment Through Physical Ambush: Educating God's Soldiers of Satan's Plot to Shatter Faith through Sickness and Disease (2019).
Spiritual Shipwreck on the Horizon: Exhorting Christians to Contend for the Faith and Comprehend the Deceitfulness of Sin (2019).
Satan Has No Authority Over God's Soldier: Illuminating Godlike Faith (2019).
God The Holy Spirit: The Conquering Power Within (2019).
Signs of the Time: Warning: Lukewarm Christianity Accepts Deception (2020).
Flesh and Spirit Conflict: The Inner Battle of Choice (2020).
Supernatural Faith Disables: Quench the Fiery Darts (2020).
Seeds of Knowledge: Soil Determines The Seed's Harvest (2020).

Fiction

The Elfdins and the Gold Temple: An Oralee Chronicle (2018).
Charlie McGee and the Leprechaun: Life's Curious Twist of Events (2019).
The Shrines of Manitoba: Dark Secrets Shall Be Brought to Light (2019).
Guilty as Blood: One Can Make A Difference (2019).
Back From The Dead: Light Shines as the Noonday Sun (2020).
Nazis, Holocaust, and Self-Love: Unbridled Bigotry (2020).
Chateau de Paix: Nightmare Hiding In Paradise (2020).
The Elfdins and the Gold Cross: An Oralee Chronicle: Book 2 (2021).

An Incorruptible Crown

Perseverance Conquers All Impediments

R. C. JETTE

RESOURCE *Publications* • Eugene, Oregon

AN INCORRUPTIBLE CROWN
Perseverance Conquers All Impediments

Copyright © 2021 R.C. Jette. All rights reserved. Except for brief quotations in critical publications or reviews, no part of this book may be reproduced in any manner without prior written permission from the publisher. Write: Permissions, Wipf and Stock Publishers, 199 W. 8th Ave., Suite 3, Eugene, OR 97401.

All Scriptures references are taken from the KING JAMES VERSION (KJV): KING JAMES VERSION, public domain.

Resource Publications
An Imprint of Wipf and Stock Publishers
199 W. 8th Ave., Suite 3
Eugene, OR 97401

www.wipfandstock.com

PAPERBACK ISBN: 978-1-6667-1970-3
HARDCOVER ISBN: 978-1-6667-1971-0
EBOOK ISBN: 978-1-6667-1972-7

This book is dedicated to my Lord Jesus Christ in whom I live and move and have my being.

To my husband (Paul) who is my comrade at arms.

My daughter (Dawn) to whom words cannot convey my love and gratitude.

My daughter (Christina), my son (PJ), my grandchildren (Andrew, Matthew, Joshua, Kierra, and Sarah who is with the Lord), my cousins (Mike and Susanna), and all who have helped me on my journey to that city which hath foundations whose builder and maker is God.

My special thanks is given to Wipf and Stock Publishers for their continued publication of my books under their Resource Publications.

I am grateful to Joe Delahanty, Jim Tedrick, Kara Barlow, Ian Creeger, Stephanie Randels, and Jonathan Hill.

Special mention must be given to Matthew Wimer, George Callihan, Shannon Carter, and Savanah N. Landerholm for their forbearance to get the books published.

And every man that striveth for the mastery is temperate in all things. Now they do it to obtain a corruptible crown; but we an incorruptible.

— 1 Corinthians 9:25

Contents

Introduction		ix
Chapter 1	The Cross of Self-Denial	1
Chapter 2	Conquer Selfishness	7
Chapter 3	Fire Uncovers Hidden Serpents	15
Chapter 4	Deception of Hearing Only	25
Chapter 5	Fear Subjugates Faith	34
Chapter 6	Perseverance Conquers Weariness	39
Chapter 7	Balance the Impediment	48
Chapter 8	Follow the Directions	56
Chapter 9	The War Within	67
Chapter 10	A New Horizon	76
Chapter 11	An Incorruptible Crown	81

Introduction

RECENTLY, I HAVE BEEN contemplating why Christians start the race for an incorruptible crown and then gradually turn our attention from the eternal (immortal) to the temporal (mortal). I realize the turmoil and unrest in our Nation has many uprooted and in turmoil. We seem to be focused upon the earthly with its corruptible prize. In doing so, we are becoming weary and are losing the desire to keep running.

We have forgotten what we are running for. We have forgotten why we entered the race. We have forgotten our race is lifelong. It is not like the athletes who strive to win a single race to win a corruptible prize and then go about their life. Our race is lifelong; it is never-ending while we have breath.

We have forgotten we are not running for a corruptible crown that will fade away. We have forgotten we chose to run this race because we desired to win an incorruptible crown. We have forgotten what Christ suffered to enable us to run this race. We have forgotten the power of the cross to conquer. We have forgotten we live, and move, and have our being in Christ.

We are weary of the restricted lifestyle upon our flesh. We have become more concerned with enjoying this life's pleasures instead of running for the crown of the future. Because we are centered on the now and not the future, we have lost the desire to persevere. We are focused upon this life and are being enticed daily to meander onto the wide and broad path that liberates our flesh.

Anytime we focus on other than our race, Christ, and his word, we will succumb to the pressure of the impediment we are facing. We will be overcome by its stress and sink like Peter when he took his eyes off Christ and gazed at the storm.

Overcoming the impediments of this life requires tenacity. It necessitates a determined perseverance that no matter what is coming our way, we will not succumb to Satan's diabolical strategies to destroy our faith in him who gave his life for us to be victorious. We will not surrender to our flesh which instigates us to quit because of the long and arduous race we have entered.

When we forget we have a **daily** battle that consists of combatting self with its lust of the flesh, the lust of the eyes, and the pride of life, as well as an unrelenting enemy who is bent on destroying us and our faith, we tend to become overwhelmed. We forget we can do all things through Christ which strengtheneth us (Philippians 4:13). We forget God gives us the victory through our Lord Jesus Christ (1 Corinthians 15:57). We forget all things are possible to him that believeth (Mark 9:23).

It seems forgetfulness has many focusing on the struggles, hardships, grief, heartache, turmoil, etc. of our life. Because of this, our cross of self-denial has become too cumbersome, too burdensome and our race too arduous, too demanding.

Such forgetfulness is causing us to make compromising and wrong choices in our life. We are not standing against the evil trying to overtake our life, our family, and our Nation. We have become lethargic or slothful through the laborious battle to overcome. Because of battle fatigue, we have begun to concede instead of persevering.

As I stated in my other books, many Christians seem to be ignorant of Satan's devices, schemes, methods. Such ignorance leads to defeat. This is clearly seen in the natural. If our military does not have proper intelligence about an enemy, it could be disastrous. In the spiritual, if we are not studying God's word, we will not have proper intelligence. Through a knowledge of the word of God, and

INTRODUCTION

being sensitive to the prompting of the Holy Spirit, we will be enabled to avoid defeat.

I believe if God's Soldiers would change our mindset, we could conquer all impediments. Instead of focusing upon the impediments of storms, struggles, trials, hardships, grief, etc., we need to focus upon why we are in this race. We are not in it for the pleasures of this life that will all fade away. We are in this race for an incorruptible crown promised to all who denied self, had self-control, and brought their body unto subjection to the will of God.

Prayerfully, reading this book will help encourage any who are feeling overwhelmed, defeated, and discouraged to comprehend overcoming all impediments in this life is determined through perseverance. It is the never surrender mentality that will cause us to vanquish whatever impediments of storms, obstacles, strategies, etc. the enemy hurls our way.

The purpose for this book is to ignite the fire in us to persevere and focus on our eternal glory and not this life. We will be encouraged to keep running as we remember our light afflictions of this life are for a season, whereas receiving our incorruptible crown is forever.

Listen to me, be encouraged. No matter what you are facing at present, it is only for a season. God has equipped you through his Holy Spirit to conquer whatever comes your way. If you feel overwhelmed, it is because you are ill prepared through a lack of knowledge. However, such ignorance can be easily rectified through a knowledge of your ability in Christ. As you read through these chapters, you will be educated and enlightened to focus not on the impediments, but concentrate on an incorruptible crown that awaits your final conquest!

Chapter 1

The Cross of Self-Denial

23)And he said to them all, If any man will come after me, let him deny himself, and take up his cross daily, and follow me. 24)For whosoever will save his life shall lose it: but whosoever will lose his life for my sake, the same shall save it. (Luke 9:23 – 24)

BEFORE WE START EXPLAINING the importance of perseverance and its necessity to conquer impediments crucial to receiving an incorruptible crown, we must comprehend what cross we are to carry daily.

Many claim to be carrying our cross because of this or that. We speak about it as if we are some sort of martyr to be praised for such an endeavor. We expect to be applauded for our effort by family, friends, co-workers, etc. We react like the Pharisee in Luke 18:10 – 14 all puffed up in our pride and self-righteousness and ignore our sinful nature. Whereas we need to be the publican who smites our breast at the reality of who and what we really are. We should be grateful for the honor to be his servant taking up our cross.

> So likewise ye, when ye shall have done all those things which are commanded you, say, We are unprofitable servants: we have done that which was our duty to do. (Luke 17:10)

No matter what we do for the Lord in obedience to his word, we have done no more than what is our duty to do. Taking up our cross daily is our moral obligation, our responsibility, what is required of us if we are followers of Jesus Christ. Thinking we deserve special honor for being in obedience puts us in the category of the prideful and sanctimonious Pharisee (Luke 18:9 – 14).

Since the creation of man, there have always been extremes. However, our time seems to be the epitome of excesses. Man no longer abides by moral standards that were upheld not too many years ago. Much extremism was kept in restraint, because unrestraint was unacceptable by most.

Today, mankind flaunts sin like a badge or some sort of banner to be proud of. I mean, look at the gay pride parades waving their banner applauding what the Word of God condemns (Leviticus 18:22; 20:13). Sin has been unleashed without restrictions. Corruption, wickedness, evil are so rampant that morality and religion seem to be non-existent at times.

Now, the sad reality in this looseness of restraint is those claiming to be God's soldiers have joined the depravity. Look around and see some who sit in church on Sunday are living in adultery, fornication, homosexuality, gossip, lying, etc. Many have ceased from being doers of the word, and are content to be hearers only. We are deceived into believing we are following Christ, when we are in stride with the world following the devil.

Denying self and taking up our cross is believed by many to be self-imprisonment. Instead of taking up our cross, we listen to itching ear preachers claiming Jesus denied himself so we do not have to. He desires us to live an abundant life. He wants us to be happy. Denying self is not an abundant life, but one of confinement.

The Cross of Self-Denial

How has this wickedness occurred? Why are many who claim a relationship with Christ living such lives? What happened to holiness, righteousness, and godliness that is supposed to be named among us who name the name of Christ?

The answer is found in our scripture text in Luke. In those verses, Jesus gave the secret or the key to self-deliverance. Sin in our life is the result of self-indulgence. The world has no desire to restrain its fleshly appetites. It has no intention of denying self its lust of the flesh, the lust of the eyes, and the pride of life to follow Jesus. It has no desire to walk the straight and narrow way to life.

God's soldiers are supposed to be his followers. However, the lives of many reveal we are not following Christ. Self-indulgence is never the result of pursuing a relationship with the Savior. The only way for us to follow Jesus is to deny self on a daily basis. If we are indulging our flesh (self) we are not following Jesus. If we are in disobedience to his word, we are not following Christ. We cannot claim to be a follower of Jesus Christ when we ignore the Word of God, follow our desires, and give into what our flesh wants and obey it.

God will have no other gods before him (Exodus 20:3). What does that mean? It suggests nothing or no one is to take priority before our worship, obedience, or service to God. If we live in sin of any kind, we have chosen self to be our god. If we love a person who takes precedence over obedience to God's word, that person is our god. If we choose to defile the temple of the Holy Ghost through drug or alcohol abuse, that substance becomes our god.

If Jesus is our Lord and Savior, we have chosen to believe God's word, have committed ourselves to follow him no matter the cost to our flesh. This requires a daily self-denial and a willingness to ignore what we want and choose his will. It will be a daily battle to keep the old man dead with Christ.

To take up our cross daily is to expect distressing situations each day because of our fidelity to Christ. Too many Christians are not preparing themselves for daily hardships and when things get tough, we are either the wayside of rejecting God's word, the stony ground that cannot take the heat of persecution, or we allow the thorns to choke the word because of the cares of this world, the deceitfulness of riches, or the lusts of other things (lust of the flesh, lust of the eyes, or the pride of life).

If anything or anyone takes precedence over obedience to God and his word, we are not following Jesus and He is not our God. He showed us how to take up our cross of self-denial. His cross of self-denial has given us the opportunity to be his child. None of us will ever have to carry such a heavy cross. None of us will have to deny self and be separated from God in order to become man's sin and receive God's judgment for the sins of others.

> 17)*For our light affliction, which is but for a moment, worketh for us a far more exceeding and eternal weight of glory; 18)While we look not at the things which are seen, but at the things which are not seen: for the things which are seen are temporal; but the things which are not seen are eternal. (2 Corinthians 4:17 – 18)*

As long as God's soldiers focus upon the temporal or the pleasures of this world, we will never take up our cross of self-denial. We will reject its heaviness, because it restrains, inhibits our flesh.

All that is in this world will one day be no more (2 Peter 3:10). With that reality, we should strive to be holy in conversation and godliness looking for and hasting the coming of the day of God (2 Peter 3:11 – 12).

We must stop living for this world which will burn up. We must grasp whatever impediments needed to persevere in this life are **light** compared to the glory awaiting us with Christ. Once we comprehend the impediments of this life are but a moment, we choose to focus on the eternal weight of glory. We choose to look not at the things which are seen, but at the things which are not seen.

Our focus veers from the temporal and fixes itself upon the eternal. We concentrate upon our incorruptible crown and eternity with Christ. When that occurs, our mindset is to take up our cross daily no matter how heavy or how painful upon our flesh.

Desiring that crown must be the craving of our life. If it is not, there will be no self-denial. In chapter six, I mention about

The Cross of Self-Denial

the self-denial of athletes. Here, I am concerned with clarifying the cross required for God's soldiers to carry. If we do not deny self and take up our cross daily, we will not receive our incorruptible crown. Only he that overcomes this life will inherit all things and God will be our God and we his child (Revelation 21:7).

Jesus claims if we are to come after him, we must deny self, take up our cross daily, and follow him. Only as we deny self can we obey God's word and resist the lust of the flesh, the lust of the eyes, and the pride of life. The cross of self-denial is the cross we must choose to take up daily if we are to follow Christ. We cannot claim to be a follower of Christ if we are not denying self and taking up our heavy cross daily.

The cross weighs heavy because we are taking up that which is in opposition to what our flesh wants. It is the old battle of the spirit against the flesh that must be fought daily (Galatians 5:17). However, if we do not willingly take it up, we will never persevere and conquer all impediments that could hinder us from receiving our incorruptible crown.

Let me help us understand what taking up our heavy cross of self-denial accomplishes. We cannot do good to our enemies without taking up the heavy cross of self-denial. We cannot love the unlikeable without taking up the heavy cross of self-denial. We cannot forgive what is overwhelming without taking up the heavy cross of self-denial. We cannot do the word which is opposite of what our flesh desires without taking up the heavy cross of self-denial.

Our whole Christian life will consist of doing what our flesh does not want to do. We cannot do what is uncomfortable, painful, distressing upon our flesh without the cross of self-denial. That is why Jesus said *if any man will come after me, let him deny himself, and take up his cross daily, and follow me.* He knew we could never do what is necessary to conquer the impediments of this life without taking up our cross of self-denial daily.

> 24)*Of the Jews five times received I forty stripes save one.*
> 25)*Thrice was I beaten with rods, once was I stoned, thrice I suffered shipwreck, a night and a day I have been in the*

> *deep; 26)In journeyings often, in perils of waters, in perils or robbers, in perils by mine own countrymen, in perils by the heathen, in perils in the city, in perils in the wilderness, in perils in the sea, in perils among false brethren; 27)In weariness and painfulness, in watchings often, in hunger and thirst, in fastings often, in cold and nakedness. 28) Besides those things that are without, that which cometh upon me daily, the care of all the churches. (2 Corinthians 11:24 – 28)*

Besides Jesus, a good example of taking up his heavy cross of self-denial is found in the Apostle Paul. Some of his impediments are listed in above verses. How many of God's soldiers would carry such a heavy cross of self-denial daily? How many of us would claim to be content with such a heavy cross of self-denial (Philippians 4:11)? How many of us bicker and complain whenever we are required to deny self? How many have not yet realized receiving an incorruptible crown is contingent upon our disciplining our body or having self-control?

God's word is efficacious. It is able to perform what He ordained it to do. When it does not, it is due to our lack of taking up our cross of self-denial. When we do not deny self, God's word of promise cannot be fulfilled in our lives.

Remember our iniquities separate us from him, and our sins hide his face from us, that He will not hear (Isaiah 59:2). Are we rejecting self-denial because of the restraint upon our flesh? Are we missing out on the promises of God because we quit carrying the cross of self-denial?

Our cross will always become heavy when we must do something our flesh will recoil, cower, or cringe to do. Doing what is in opposition to our old nature will take stamina or perseverance. Without the agony on our flesh of daily taking up our heavy cross of self-denial, we will not receive an incorruptible crown!

Chapter 2

Conquer Selfishness

32)And he took again the twelve, and began to tell them what things should happen unto him, 33)saying, Behold, we go up to Jerusalem; and the Son of man shall be delivered unto the chief priests, and unto the scribes; and they shall condemn him to death, and shall deliver him to the Gentiles; 34)and they shall mock him, and shall scourge him, and shall spit upon him, and shall kill him: and the third day he shall rise again. 35) And James and John, the sons of Zebedee, come unto him, saying, Master, we would that thou shouldest do for us whatsoever we shall desire. 36)And he said unto them, What would ye that I should do for you? 37)They said unto him, Grant unto us that we may sit, one on thy right hand, and the other on thy left hand, in thy glory. 38)But Jesus said unto them, Ye know not what ye ask: can ye drink of the cup that I drink of? and be baptized with the baptism that I am baptized with? 39) And they said unto him, We can. And Jesus said unto them, Ye shall indeed drink of the cup that I drink of; and with the baptism that I am baptized withal shall

ye be baptized: 40)but to sit on my right hand and on my left hand is not mine to give; but it shall be given to them for whom it is prepared. 41)And when the ten heard it, they began to be much displeased with James and John. 42)But Jesus called them to him, and saith unto them, Ye know that they which are accounted to rule over the Gentiles exercise lordship over them; and their great ones exercise authority upon them. 43)But so shall it not be among you: but whosoever will be great among you, shall be your minister: 44)and whosoever of you will be the chiefest, shall be servant of all.
(Mark 10: 32 - 44)

MANKIND IS PRONE TO selfishness through self-worship. Selfishness will not deny self any self-gratification. This is obvious all around us. Many want to be god of their life. To be god of one's life is the desire to be in control, to be noticed, to receive accolades, to be answerable to none. It means pleasing self and pleasing others as long as it gratifies self.

Man wants to be worshipped. Why is there so many aiming to be famous, to be a celebrity, to be rich, etc.? Whether it is seeking to be a movie star, singer, top person of the company, desire for awards, fame, fortune, etc. Whatever it is, people want to be noticed, get recognition, be bragged about, adored, or worshipped.

Several years ago, I read in World Magazine that Hollywood gets Religion, but the evangelism in *Seven Years in Tibet* was for Buddhism. As if the celebrities are not recognized or famous enough, they want to be a god. Why do I say that? Because Buddhism teaches you can become a god.

> 1)*Vanity of vanities, saith the preacher, vanity of vanities; all is vanity. 9)The thing that hath been, it is that which shall be; and that which is done is that which shall be done: and there is no new thing under the sun. (Ecclesiastes 1:2,9)*

Conquer Selfishness

Man's inner ego or self-pride is no new thing. Eastern religion and so called New Age religions are not new. To find man seeking vanity, accolades, praise, etc. has been occurring since man's creation.

Look at the temptation of Adam and Eve in the Garden of Eden. Was it not their desire to be like God? Was it not their desire to be placed at the level of God that enticed them to eat the forbidden fruit or disobey God's word?

Sometimes, we tend to think the conceited, proud, braggard is what vanity describes. They seem to be obvious. However, the longer I walk with God, I see it can also be the so called one with the low self-image. He/she spends more time in selfishness than the one who appears to be self-centered.

We are forever grieving the Holy Spirit by our constant pity party. The "me" syndrome reigns in us because all our thoughts center upon self. We are so self-centered that we cannot think of anything but our blunder, our misfortune, our grievance, etc.

Any time we spend more thought on ourselves, we are selfish. If we would be honest, we can see dwelling on our blunder, our misfortune, our grievance, etc. is being self-centered. If we are self-centered, we are selfish. We need to be like the one who falls off his bike, gets up, dusts off, and gets back on the bike until we conquer the impediment. We cannot vanquish anything without perseverance. It is a constant battle of falling, getting up, and riding until we overcome.

In our scripture text in Mark, we need to take a closer look at verses thirty-two through thirty-four. In those scriptures, Jesus has just told the disciples He is to be condemned to death. He was to be delivered to the Gentiles who would mock him, spit on him, and crucify him.

The Gentiles or Romans used crucifixion for non-Romans, for it was a slow, painful death. If you remember, Paul was beheaded. Because he was a Roman citizen, his death would be swift. Because Jesus was Jewish, and not a citizen of Rome, He would be crucified.

Anyway, Jesus is in agony, He knows what is to befall him when He goes to Jerusalem. I know the disciples, on a few occasions, have wrongly responded to Jesus. Like when He told them to beware of the leaven of the Pharisees, and they thought it was because they brought no bread (Matthew 16:15 – 21).

I must admit James and John's response to Jesus' revelation here tops them all. Think of this. It seems uncanny. How can we even comprehend Jesus predicting the horror to take place at Jerusalem could be followed by such self-serving bickering?

But here it is in black and white, the selfishness of his disciples. They should have went into prayer to not enter into temptation. But no they did not, as is the case in many of his disciples today. We ignore anything to deny self in our quest for selfishness.

Their minds were on self-gratification, self-glory. So incensed with the "me" syndrome. Yes, Matthew chapter twenty claims it was their mother. Whether the idea originated with them or their mother is irrelevant. Because in both Gospels, Jesus does not address the mother, but them. Jesus knew their hearts and both desired and sought for such a prominent position.

Granted they had not yet sold out for the Lord, but that is the crux of the matter. If we are not sold out one hundred percent for Christ, we will be more concerned about self than God's will for our life. We will, as the disciples, be self-centered. Our selfish want will interfere with what God is trying to reveal to us.

Let me continue to unfold this. I want us to think how repugnant to their best interest this was. They had been called by Jesus from being fishermen to learn or acquire spiritual knowledge. Yet, they were looking or seeking honor and glory for themselves. How terribly like Satan (who is the god of self-seeking). The devil had blinded their eyes and deluded their hearts. How many of us have allowed the devil to blind our eyes and delude our hearts to truth because of selfishness, what I want, what I desire, and ignore the word of God?

I want to make clear here concerning the other disciples. Although only two asked this request, the others revealed by their indignation to James and John they were under the influence of the same selfish ambition.

Conquer Selfishness

How many of us are like James and John today? How many of us hear only what we want to hear? How many of us listen with our own desires or motives at heart? How many of us allow selfishness to rule our heart? How many of us interpret the word to fall in line with our selfish desires?

Jesus has just given reference to his Messianic title "Son of Man' and coupled it with Jerusalem. Refusing to deal with the core of Jesus' statements, all James and John heard was *and the third day he shall rise again.*

To their minds, it was the vision of a potent, ruling Messianic Son of Man. Yet, Jesus' graphic details of an immediate future filled with condemnation, rejection, mocking, spitting, scourging, and execution, had no impression on James and John. Instead of humility, they approach Jesus with a foolish and self-serving question.

Jesus' sharp response of *ye know not what ye ask* reveals the ignorance and arrogance of these two disciples. He was saying if you had been led by the Spirit, you would have never asked for self-glory. But since you are led of self, you have no idea of the malicious intent of your self-seeking. Self-seeking will blind us to the true motive of what we desire. Selfishness will stifle our faith walk and our ability to conquer impediments.

Then Jesus asks them *can ye drink of the cup that I drink of? And be baptized with the baptism that I am baptized with?* As we ponder those questions, what is He saying? Jesus is revealing the path which leads to such exalted positions in which we may not have considered closely enough.

Those two questions contain images to convey the essence of channels to glorification. The cup has a long tradition in Hebrew Scripture as the cup filled with divine wrath and judgment from which disobedient humanity must drink.

For Jesus to drink of "the cup" is his voluntary drinking of God's judgment for our sake. Jesus drank the cup intended for us.

Let me explain more explicitly. We (you and me) deserve God's wrath for our sins. However, when we repent or turn away (a 180 degree turn) from our sins, we receive God forgiveness instead of his wrath. Jesus conquered selfishness and partook of God's cup of wrath for us. He did not complain that we were the ones who sinned and not him. He loved us so much that He willingly took our place for the punishment due us for our sins.

How many of us would willingly suffer the punishment due someone else? How many of us would willingly die for someone else who committed a crime? Let us be truthful. We are not willing to let someone have the last cookie, etc.

God soldiers are selfish in so many ways. We want the last word. We want to be praised. We want to own that expensive car. We want the finest house. We want the best of everything. Whereas Jesus became a servant to save us from God's wrath. How many of us have the servant mentality?

When Jesus referred to baptism, He is most likely recalling the rites practiced by John the Baptist which is a baptism of repentance. As a symbol of repentance, baptism becomes linked, like the cup, to the divine judgment awaiting human sinfulness.

By participating in a repentant act of baptism, Jesus again took upon himself the judgment humanity deserves. The fact James and John were unhesitantly willing to share in Jesus' cup and baptism reveals how little they understood the personal cost that lies behind these paths. Jesus had to deny self and choose the path of suffering. It is the path of denying self, taking up our heavy cross of self-denial daily, and following Jesus (Luke 9:23). If we are to follow the path of Jesus, we must pay the cost of denying self whatever it wants. It is a mindset upon perseverance that will deny self and conquer whatever impediment we face.

Many claiming to be Christians consider the daily carrying of the cross too hindering to our liberty. To take up our cross means a daily crucifixion of our fleshly desires. Selfishness is rooted deeply in us, and we find denying self what it craves too costly. We will never conquer sin unless we deny self. To overcome, selfishness must be subdued or restrained.

In verse forty-one, we see the other ten self-seekers. Jesus now has twelve self-seeking disciples. At this, He informs them they are acting like Gentiles or heathens who do not know God.

Conquer Selfishness

Jesus told them there is only one way to greatness in God's kingdom. It is not through self-seeking or selfishness. It is only through service that one may become great. The lowlier and servant like the service, the greater the genuine stature of the disciple.

By his own example, Jesus showed us this. He, who, is God Almighty, the Alpha and the Omega made himself of no reputation, but took upon himself the form of a servant, and was made in the likeness of sinful man (Philippians 2:7). Instead of appearing in outward pomp and splendor, He lowered himself in the likeness of man and came to minister unto his own rebellious creatures.

> But God commendeth his love toward us, in that, while we were yet sinners, Christ died for us. (Romans 5:8)

Jesus not only spent his life in the service of mankind, but laid down his life for us to ransom our souls from death and Hell. No sacrifice to self was too great for him to make for our welfare, no suffering too heavy for him to persevere. His love for us knew know bounds. We cannot comprehend such love that would willingly die for his enemies. While we were sinners, we were the enemies of God.

> 4)Surely he hath borne our griefs, and carried our sorrows: yet we did esteem him stricken, smitten of God, and afflicted. 5)But he was wounded for our transgressions, he was bruised for our iniquities: the chastisement of our peace was upon him; and with his stripes we are healed. (Isaiah 53:4 – 5)

He bore our infirmities, our sorrows, our sins in his own body on the tree; enduring in his person the curse due us, that we might inherit eternal blessedness. That is the epitome of being unselfish or selflessness.

As we understand how unselfish Jesus was, it should be the height of our ambition to mimic him. It should be our ultimate goal to conquer selfishness in our life. It should be our central focus to stay fixed upon our incorruptible crown and persevere until we conquer all impediments of this life.

We have read this chapter, but will we leave it as James and John to seek self-gratification, self-recognition, selfishness in whatever form pleases our flesh? Will we ponder its truths and accept the fact, the channel, the path, the road, the way to everlasting life requires us to conquer the impediment of selfishness? Conquering selfishness requires perseverance. We alone decide to deny self its lust of the flesh, the lust of the eyes, and the pride life.

God does not divide us into two groups. We have been given a free-will to choose whether we are part of the selfish group or selfless group. If we choose to conquer selfishness, we choose to persevere, conquer all impediments, and receive an incorruptible crown!

Chapter 3

Fire Uncovers Hidden Serpents

2)And the barbarous people shewed us no little kindness: for they kindled a fire, and received us every one, because of the present rain, and because of the cold. 3) And when Paul had gathered a bundle of sticks, and laid them on the fire, there came a viper out of the heat, and fastened on his hand. (Acts 28:2 – 3)

WITHOUT THE HOLY GHOST fire, we will never know what is actually hiding in our flesh waiting to spring forth. How can we conquer what we are unaware of? We need the fire like nature needs sunshine to grow and flourish.

For us to comprehend this truth, I have broken it down into four sections or four points of *Provision, Production, Perception, and Perseverance*. In doing this, we will be enabled to understand why we need to face the impediments of storms, obstacles, trials, and strategies of Satan in this life to overcome. Accepting this fact, provides us with the power to persevere until we have conquered all impediments.

Only the fire can bring forth the chaff or hidden serpents to be eliminated. As we grasp the fire's purpose and need, we are encouraged to press forward, to deny self, to persevere, and to run the race that is set before us, because we are focused on an incorruptible crown.

PROVISION

> *But my God shall supply all your* need *according to his riches in glory by Christ Jesus. (Philippians 4:19)*

First of all, we must realize God supplies or provides (meaning his provision) all our need. Most of us look at need as money, house, car, job, food, clothes, etc. While this is true, most of God's soldiers do not realize a need in the Greek is also a requirement needed or depended on for success of fulfillment.

> 6)*Wherein ye greatly rejoice, though now for a season, if need be, ye are in heaviness through manifold temptations:* 7)*That the trial of your faith, being much more precious than of gold that perisheth, though it be tried with fire, might be found unto praise and honour and glory at the appearing of Jesus Christ. (1 Peter 1:6 – 7)*

In the above verses, Peter informs us for a season (a time), we are in heaviness or distress through manifold or various, multiple temptations (impediments of storms, obstacles, strategies, trials) *if need be*. It is imperative to understand these tests are **needed**; they are a requirement for the trial of our faith.

Verse seven makes evident our faith is tried by fire if it is going to be much more precious than gold. Why must our faith be tried by fire? If not, it will not be found unto praise and honor and glory when Christ appears or returns.

Only faith tried or tested with fire will be found without alloys. The fire will bring out a faith more precious than gold. It will bring forth a faith fortified to persevere whatever impediment comes our way.

Fire Uncovers Hidden Serpents

Now, we see it is God who provides the fire required or needed to assess the strength or validity of our faith. God promises to supply all we need.

When God supplies or provides all our need or requirement, it includes the fire to test the purity, the sincerity of our faith. We must understand the provision of fire is necessary for our faith to be examined. Without the fire, our faith will never be pure, be strengthened, be like gold, be found unto praise, and honor, and glory when Christ returns.

Once we grasp the truth that fire is provided by God to turn up the heat, we are ready for production.

PRODUCTION

> *14)But not long after there arose against it a tempestuous wind, called Euroclydon. 20)And when neither sun nor stars in many days appeared, and no small tempest lay on us, all hope that we should be saved was then taken away. 29)Then fearing lest we should have fallen upon rocks, they cast four anchors out of the stern, and wished for the day. 33)And while the day was coming, on, Paul besought them all to take meat, saying, This day is the fourteenth day that ye have tarried and continued fasting, having taken nothing. 41) And falling into a place where two seas met, they ran the ship aground; and the forepart stuck fast, and remained unmoveable, but the hinder part was broken with the violence of the waves. 44) and the rest, some on boards, and some on broken pieces of the ship. And so it came to pass, that they escaped all safe to land. (Acts 27:14,20,29, 33, 41,44)*

In Acts chapter twenty-seven, we see Paul and the others had to persevere an arduous journey. They fasted fourteen days, fought tumultuous winds, the ship is destroyed, land on a strange island, worn out, probably feeling more dead than alive, and still enduring rain and cold.

To help them, the barbarians kindle them a fire to warm up. This is where we understand *production* or what is produced during the trial or testing by fire. This also helps us to see why the need or requirement for fire is essential to spiritual maturity. Also, we see God's provision of a fire.

We saw in 1 Peter the fire is required to test our faith. Now, God is revealing in Acts that ONLY in the hot fire of testing can what is inside (hiding away in the inner recesses of our heart) come out.

Fire produces what is hidden. Without the fire, there is no production. The fire brings to surface what is concealed in the deep reserves within us. We have no idea what is hiding in our flesh until the fire is turned up. We are ignorant of the serpent, something destructive, something deadly hiding inside all of our carnal nature (our fleshly man).

This truth was revealed to me as a young Christian. As I meditated upon Dr. Jekyll and Mr. Hyde. I do not remember whether it was a movie or what, however, the revelation stunned me. The Holy Ghost revealed Dr. Jekyll is the Christian walking in the spirit (the new nature), and Mr. Hyde is the Christian walking in the flesh (the old nature). You see Dr. Jekyll and Mr. Hyde are the same person with two reactions or two natures.

Any time we give into our old nature, the hideous, evil monster comes forth. As we learn to walk by faith through the trials by fire, the more we keep the monster controlled.

Listen to me. It is imperative for God's soldiers to comprehend once we are born again, we have two natures. How many times have we felt like we are two people? It is because we are. Our new nature reacts like Christ, and our old nature reacts like the devil. It is like Dr. Jekyll and Mr. Hyde.

> 16)This I say then, Walk in the Spirit, and ye shall not fulfill the lust of the flesh. 17)For the flesh lusteth against the Spirit, and the Spirit against the flesh: and these are contrary the one to the other: so that ye cannot do the things that ye would. (Galatians 5:16 – 17)

Fire Uncovers Hidden Serpents

The battlefield is within us, and the conflict will continue the rest of our lives. It is a lifelong struggle of choosing whether we yield to sin's control, or whether we surrender to the Spirit's demand to continue under Christ's authority. Only as we yield to the Holy Ghost will we be enabled to conquer our own ungodly desires and dominate the urges of the sinful nature.

> 22)*That ye put off concerning the former conversation the old man, which is corrupt according to the deceitful lusts:* 23)*And be renewed in the spirit of your mind;* 24)*And that ye put on the new man, which after God is created in righteousness and true holiness. (Ephesians 4:22 – 24)*

Putting off the corruption of the old man takes time, effort, determination, and commitment. It requires lifelong perseverance. As our mind is renewed, we put on the new man. Again, this takes time, effort, determination, and commitment.

It can be a long, arduous journey as Paul and the others in the ship. To renew our mind means to read and study our Bible, be under sound biblical teaching, prayer, fasting, etc. It means we no longer hang out with people who are not saved. We no longer go to places that will not encourage the renewal of our mind. We must with all perseverance put off the former conversation (the way we spoke, the way we thought, and the way we lived). Simply put, it is daily denying self, daily putting off the old man, daily carrying the heavy cross of self-denial, and daily putting on the new man. This is only accomplished by daily renewing our mind.

Now, the provision of the fire produces what is really inside. We have no idea what is hiding in our flesh. The more carnal we are, the more Mr. Hyde (that deadly destructive serpent) is revealed. He manifests in anger, jealousy, panic attacks, lying, scheming, frustration, outbursts of foul language, envy, lust of the flesh, etc. Whereas the more we put on the new man and are led by the Spirit, the less and less is seen of Mr. Hyde (our carnal nature).

Without God providing the fire, we will never conquer the serpent, the monster, Mr. Hyde which is our old nature. Once we comprehend the need of the fire is to produce God's will, we are ready for perception.

PERCEPTION

And we know that all things work together for good to them that love God, to them who are the called according to his purpose. (Romans 8:28)

Our perception, our understanding, our insight is how we decipher this trial by fire. The way in which we perceive the storm, obstacle, strategy, etc. determines our reaction, our response. Our perception affects how we reciprocate or respond. Whether we persevere is contingent upon our perception of God and his will.

The key to coming through the trial by fire being found unto praise, honor, and glory is our perception. If we perceive something negatively, we will reciprocate negatively. If we perceive something positively, we will reciprocate positively.

Our scripture text in Romans reveals all things work together for the good to those who love God and are in his will. We must believe God will bring good out of all impediments of storms, obstacles, difficulties, troubles, persecution, grief, suffering, etc. Not that He will change the impediments themselves, but good will come out through the impediments or the fiery furnace. As we come through the fire, we will become more like Jesus. Our faith will become stronger and more resilient against trials.

As we perceive this is God's will for my life, we reciprocate or react in the positive. That is why we need to read and study his word. The more understanding of his word, the more we know and understand God. An understanding of God or how we perceive God will determine our perception of the trial by fire.

If you have read my other books, especially *Storms Are Faith's Workout*, you know how an understanding of God's love for us is vital to overcoming the trial by fire. Unless we comprehend his love, we will never trust him. Only as we trust in his love, trust in his divine plan for our life, will we trust and rest in his grace. Without that foundation, we will fail during the trial by fire.

Proper perception is facilitated by knowing God loves us. We must not waiver in the belief that He loves us. Doubting God's love will never permit us to perceive all that He is doing in our life is out of his perfect love or for our good.

Once we perceive the trial by fire is good for our life and is God's will, we are ready for perseverance.

PERSEVERANCE

> 57)But thanks be to God, which giveth us the victory through our Lord Jesus Christ. 58)Therefore, my beloved brethren, be ye steadfast, unmoveable, always abounding in the work of the Lord, forasmuch as ye know that your labour is not in vain in the Lord. (1 Corinthians 15: 57 – 58)

How we perceive determines whether we persevere or endure. If we sincerely believe God loves us and desires the best for us, then we can accept his will for our life – even in the trial by fire. The trial by fire can include losing our job, being financially overwhelmed, fighting sickness or disease, losing a loved one, rebellious children, etc. But if we believe God can be cruel and manipulating and does things for his will and not out of love for us, we will rebel in the trial by fire.

Only as we perceive the longsuffering or patience of God towards us will we decipher his love for us. God is patiently working in our life to help us become mature in our faith. Our faith cannot be purified by any other method than the trial by fire. As the dross cannot be brought up and separated from gold without fire, neither can the hidden serpent come to the surface and be separated. For gold to be pure, the impurities must be eliminated. For faith to be pure, the impurities must be eliminated. This is only acquired by fire.

> There hath no temptation taken you but such as is common to man: but God is faithful, who will not suffer you to be tempted above that ye are able; but will with the temptation also make a way to escape, that ye may be able to bear it. (1 Corinthians 10:13)

Whatever we go through, it is no new thing. All tests and trials are common to mankind. There is not any of us going through a unique trial. To think we are the only one going through such a trial is to be ignorant of scripture. God knows the amount of heat needed to eliminate the chaff or sin hindering our faith.

The way of escape does not mean the trial or test ends. When it says the way of escape, it refers to the way of escape during the trial by fire that will enable us to bear the heat, test, trial, or impediment. In the Greek, the word **bear** in the above verse means to bear from underneath, to endure. It requires perseverance through the trial by fire.

How we perceive God and trust him during the impediment of the trial is what determines our production or our fruit during the trial by fire. The time frame or season for the trial is only known by God. He gives us a promise, then comes the trial by fire. It can last years. Our example of years for a trial by fire is seen in Abraham and Sarah waiting twenty-five years for the fulfillment of the promised Isaac.

The key to perseverance during the fire is our perception. We can count on the trial by fire whenever God gives us a promise. I mention this truth in my other books. We must expect whenever we receive a promise from God (seedtime) the impediment or fiery trial will occur before the fulfillment of the promise (harvest). Without the proper perception there will be no perseverance. A proper perception always expects the storm or trial by fire between seedtime and harvest. It knows without the trial, there is no perfecting our faith. Without strengthening our faith, we will not persevere. Without perseverance, we will not conquer our flesh. Without denying self, we will not receive an incorruptible crown.

> *1)Wherefore seeing we also are compassed about with so great a cloud of witnesses, let us lay aside every weight, and the sin which doth so easily beset us, and let us run with patience the race that is set before us, 2)Looking unto Jesus the author and finisher of our faith: who for the joy that was set before him endured the cross, despising the shame, and is set down at the right hand of the throne of God. 3)*

Fire Uncovers Hidden Serpents

For consider him that endured such contradiction of sinners against himself, lest ye be wearied and faint in your minds. 4) Ye have not resisted unto blood, striving against sin. (Hebrews 12:1 – 4)

We must comprehend our race is a lifelong test of our faith. It is a life of impediments or trials by fire. The race should be run with patience or with persistent patience and perseverance. We must put aside whatever has repeatedly gotten the best of us and has kept us from growing. Only the trials by fire will enable us to keep unloading unnecessary baggage (sin, doubt, unbelief, self, hidden serpents) obstructing our race to the finish line.

If we are to persevere, like a runner who keeps his eye on the finish line, we must keep our eyes on Jesus as the goal of our faith. He is both the start and finish of our race. Since He is the author and finisher of our faith, our faith has its beginning in him and is completed in him.

Jesus did not focus on the trial by fire or the cross. He kept his eyes on the finish. When He finished, it meant a personal relationship with all who follow him. His perception was not on the suffering, but the joy of what was ahead enabled him to persevere.

When we feel ourselves becoming weary of the fire (trial, storm, obstacle, strategy) consider, contemplate, think about the sufferings of Jesus. Consider how He went through the trial by fire for us. His trial by fire was due to our sins, there was no sin in him. His suffering was because of us.

He suffered, endured, persevered such a trial by fire in which the agony caused him to sweat drops of blood. The fight against his flesh was an agony that we cannot comprehend because we who love and serve him will never have to do what He did.

In order to take on our sins, his trial by fire meant He had to be separated from the Father. Jesus suffered not only the physical abuse, but was severed from the Father whom He had been one with from eternity.

Are we willing to suffer in our flesh for the Father to bring out what is hindering us from conquering and overcoming sin in our life? Are we willing to deny self what it wants for the will of God to become a reality in our life? Only the trial by fire will accomplish his will.

In every fire, there is the possibility of a hidden serpent. We have no idea what sin may be hidden deep within. If we reject the fire, it will remain hidden until it becomes an uncontrollable monster that will consume and destroy our faith walk.

Only as we perceive the importance of conquering the hidden serpent or old nature will we persevere through each trial by fire and receive an incorruptible crown!

Chapter 4

Deception of Hearing Only

> 21)Wherefore lay apart all filthiness and superfluity of naughtiness, and receive with meekness the engrafted word, which is able to save your souls. 22)But be ye doers of the word, and not hearers only, deceiving your own selves. 23)For if any be a hearer of the word, and not a doer, he is like unto a man beholding his natural face in a glass: 24)for he beholdeth himself, and goeth his way, and straightway forgetteth what manner of man he was. 25)But whoso looketh into the perfect law of liberty, and continueth therein, he being not a forgetful hearer, but a doer of the work, this man shall be blessed in his deed. (James 1:21 – 25)

GOD'S SOLDIERS BEGIN OUR new life in Christ through being born again. It is a life transformation like the caterpillar into butterfly. This renovation changes our attitude, our thoughts, our actions. We change inside and the transformation is revealed outward.

This spiritual birth happens when we repent of sin. We admit our sin and turn away from it. We do a 180 degree turn. Our sin is now behind us. It is no longer part of our life. We cannot claim a spiritual birth without a renovation in our life. It is a complete change from our old life of sin to one of desiring to obey God and follow the leading of the Holy Spirit.

If we are being led by the Holy Spirit, we will not desire to continue in sin. We cannot remain in a right personal relationship with God unless we sincerely pursue God's purposes and vigilantly avoid evil (sin).

Can two walk together, except they be agreed? (Amos 3:3)

What Amos is revealing is we are not walking with God, if we are not in agreement with his word. The result of our sin causes us to lose our special relationship with God. As no true cooperation or companionship can exist between people without agreement on some basic issues and truths, the same is true with our relationship with God.

This truth rings loud and clear when we think of marriage. I am not saying there will not be disagreements between spouses. What I am saying is agreement on basic issues and truths is vital for harmony in a marriage. We must be of one heart and one mind by seeking the Lord for his direction, his will, and his way. If there is not, there is misery. A marriage where two walk separately is not the marriage God intended. A husband and a wife are no longer twain, but one flesh (Mark 10:8).

We will never have a true relationship with God without accepting his word which reveals his character and his purpose. If we do not accept, believe, and obey his word, we are not a true follower of him. When we accept his word, it means we agree with him and are a true follower.

It does not matter how spiritual we may speak or seem to be, if we live by principles which are immoral and follow the ways of the world, our conduct reveals there is a lack of spiritual life within us. We are **not** reflecting a life of Christlikeness.

Deception of Hearing Only

Merely professing we are religious will get us nowhere. Obvious as this truth is, it requires frequent and regular repetition by the Ministers of the Gospel to inform people about the deceitfulness of sin. How many preachers are warning their congregation to flee the sins that will not inherit the Kingdom of God? How many are encouraging people to persevere through all impediments? How many are directing people to focus on receiving an incorruptible crown through denying self?

> *Follow peace with all men, and holiness, without which no man shall see the Lord. (Hebrews 12:14)*

To help us understand sin that will not inherit the Kingdom of God, the above verse makes clear if we do not follow or possess holiness, we will NOT see the Lord. What is holiness? It is a separation or setting apart. Holiness indicates sanctity or separation from all that is sinful, impure, or morally imperfect; it is moral wholeness. It is to be morally pure, spiritually whole, separated from evil, dedicated to God, and set apart for his purpose.

If we are pursuing holiness, we live our life with the aim to be like Christ. We have a strong determination to do what He says is right according to his word as written. It is like adhering to the Constitution as written or having the Constitution adhere to what we believe. We see this truth daily in elected officials who are supposed to uphold the Constitution as written, but are doing all they can to manipulate its amendments for their benefit.

Only through holiness can we be like God. That means we abhor evil, we abstain from all appearance of evil, and we strive to be holy as He is holy (Romans 12:9, 1 Thessalonians 5:22, 1 Peter 1:16).

> *They profess that they know God; but in works they deny him, being abominable, and disobedient, and unto every good work reprobate. (Titus 1:16)*

God's displeasure is greatly provoked when people profess to have faith in Christ and claim to have a personal relationship with him, but live in defiance and rebellion against his word. If we do not demonstrate in our lives, that we truly know and love God by putting his word into action, we are abominable and disobedient.

As today, in James's days there were many who professed to know God, while in works we deny him. He is denied by our ungodly lives and our unholy character. We cannot **intentionally** disobey his word and believe we have a right relationship with God.

To believe so is to deceive ourselves. When we deceive ourselves, we hear God's word, but disobey it. We pretend to be in a right relationship with Christ, but the Holy Spirit knows we have deceived ourselves by hearing and not doing God's word.

Hearers only are recognized by our words, our actions, and our fruit that we are not the real thing. We are not pure gold. We are fake, cheap metal, gold plated pretenders.

In verse twenty-five of our scripture text, James describes the Gospel as *the perfect law of liberty*. Many look at the Gospel as a mere system of restraints. But in truth, it is a LAW OF LIBERTY.

The Gospel or Law of Liberty finds us under a worse than Egyptian bondage and proclaims liberty from our yoke of oppression. It offers pardon to those who are under the condemnation of the law and freedom from the power of sin to those to whom sin has had dominion. The Gospel rescues us from the captivity in which Satan has held us. It breaks the fetters, loosing us from the world's pleasures, that had power over us.

The Law of Liberty is to captive sinners, what the Jubilee Trumpet was to the enslaved Jews. At the sound of the trumpet, Hebrew slaves and prisoners would be freed, debts would be forgiven, and the mercies of God would be particularly manifest. Through Christ, the Law of Liberty frees us from slavery to sin, frees us from the debt that we can never pay God, and forgiveness manifests God's mercy. It gives the same impact for the imprisoned soul what the angel wrought for Peter when he loosed him from death row (Acts 12:3 – 10).

Let me be clear, although it is liberty, it is still a law. The Law of Liberty (the Gospel) can be broken as can any law. We alone decide whether to obey the Law of Liberty (the Gospel) or disobey. We alone decide if we are hearers only or doers of the word. Thus,

Deception of Hearing Only

it enjoins us to embrace the Gospel or the Law of Liberty at the peril of our souls.

Nothing can be added to the Gospel to make it more effectual. No ceremonial or moral duties can at all improve Christ's finished work. If we take anything from it, we make it void. Only the blood of Christ, not any work of ours, must be regarded as the price of redemption.

> *26)For if we sin wilfully after that we have received the knowledge of the truth, there remaineth no more sacrifice for sins, 27)But a certain fearful looking for of judgment and fiery indignation, which shall devour the adversaries. 28)He that despised Moses' law died without mercy under two or three witnesses: 29)Of how much sorer punishment, suppose ye, shall he be thought worthy, who hath trodden under foot the Son of God, and hath counted the blood of the covenant, wherewith he was sanctified, an unholy thing, and hath done despite unto the Spirit of grace? (Hebrews 10: 26 – 29)*

If we keep on sinning deliberately after we have received the knowledge of the truth, we are guilty of treading on Jesus. If we disrespect and reject his sacrifice, we act as if the blood of Christ (his sacrificial death for us) is not worthy of our loyalty. We would rather be loyal to the lust of the flesh, the lust of the eyes, and the pride of life. We choose not to persevere (deny self) and conquer the impediment hindering our receiving an incorruptible crown.

To trod under foot his blood sacrifice through the continuation of sin (being a hearer only and not a doer of his word) is to reject the only sacrifice there is that can provide access to God and keep us in a right relationship with him.

What is this all about? It simply means knowledge without obedience ends in nothing. It has accomplished the opposite of its intention.

Let me give an example. We go to medical school, have a complete knowledge of being a doctor, but do nothing with our knowledge. We can quote how to heal this or that, but never become a doctor. We have heard all that would enable us to be a benefit to the infirm, but never do it. We did not do what we heard, so our hearing yielded nothing.

How do we become hearers only? We look at our own face in a glass. For a time, we have the clearest perception of our own countenance. Every line and feature is visible, and for a while we hold that picture in our mind's eye. But when we have gone *our way* (not God's way), the whole image fades. The vividness of other objects overpower it, we become more familiar with everything else than with our own natural face.

Nothing can express the shallowness, the superficiality, the hollowness of knowledge without obedience than this in James.

Let me explain further what a hearer only of the word is. We hear the word, and we see ourselves clear. I mean, we see our old nature so well. We see our *natural face*. We see what a wretch the flesh is. We see what a stinking savor sin in our life is.

As time goes by, we go our *own way*, and forget what we really are. We start to deceive ourselves. I am not really that bad. What is so wrong with this or that? The problem is that some are fanatics about this Gospel stuff. God wants me to be happy.

> 13)*Enter ye in at the strait gate: for wide is the gate, and broad is the way, that leadeth to destruction, and many there be which go in thereat:* 14)*because strait is the gate, and narrow is the way, which leadeth unto life, and few there be that find it. (Matthew 7:13 – 14)*

Jesus is teaching in these verses not to expect many to follow him on the road which leads to everlasting life. The sad truth is few will pass through the straight and narrow gate of turning from and denying their own way in order to follow Christ. The wide and broad path is chosen by most because it indulges the flesh what it wants without adhering to the restrictions of quenching fleshly lusts that lead to death. We are no longer concerned about pleasing God, but self. It may be comfortable or pleasing on the flesh, but it will not lead unto eternal life. It will not receive an incorruptible crown.

> 3)*For the time will come when they will not endure sound doctrine; but after their own lusts shall they heap to*

Deception of Hearing Only

> *themselves teachers, having itching ears. 4)And they shall turn away their ears from the truth, and shall be turned unto fables. (2 Timothy 4:3 – 4)*

Timothy makes known how we become hearers only and no longer doers of the word. Because of the indulgence of the lust of the flesh, the lust of the eyes, and the pride of life, we will choose to indulge self and shun truth. We will accept teachers teaching what is easy on our flesh. We will stop listening to the word of God renouncing sin, warning of sin's consequences, or the fire needed to cleanse sin.

Many hearers only will gather at churches and appear to honor God, but will not tolerate true faith with its demonstration of the Holy Spirit's power, a call to moral purity, and separation from the world's ungodly practices.

Hearers only will choose eloquent and entertaining speakers who accept and approve the same self-seeking and worldly desires. The messages will reassure us that we can remain a follower of Christ, though such behavior clearly contradicts the standards and principles of God's word. We will shun the straight and narrow path that restrains the flesh and choose the wide and broad path that liberates the flesh.

> *And he said to them all, If any man will come after me, let him deny himself, and take up his cross daily, and follow me. (Luke 9:23)*

To remain a doer of the word and not a hearer requires us to deny self what it wants and take up our cross daily. What does it require? It mandates us to sacrifice ourselves daily. We crucify our flesh with its lust of the flesh, lust of the eyes, and the pride of life.

If we are to receive an incorruptible crown, we must daily choose to live for Christ and not self. Doing so can be arduous and laborious because our flesh will be tempted to take the easy path. The straight and narrow squeezes the flesh and makes it uncomfortable. Our continual choice of living for ourselves (denying Christ) or living for Christ (denying self) will determine our eternal destiny.

In order to run the race and stay the path of eternal life, we must do all we can to obey his commands, pursue his purposes, and pressing on through the impediments of our life as doers of his word. This is only accomplished as we deny self what it wants.

> *The heart is deceitful above all things, and desperately wicked: who can know it? (Jeremiah 17:9)*

> *The pride of thine heart hath deceived thee. (Obadiah 1:3)*

The heart, if not totally surrendered to God, will deceive us. It will tell us things our conscience will believe as truth when it is a lie. The heart can flatter the conscience (the mind) into believing it is in the will of God, it is serving God, and it will inherit eternal life. When in reality, it is not in the will of God, it is not serving God, and it will not inherit eternal life. It has gone its own way and is no longer walking in God's will.

I know many who heard the Gospel or the Law of Liberty and were shown their natural face, repented, and walked God's way for a season. As long as they remained in the Law of Liberty (looking into the glass beholding their natural man), they were doers of the word. In time, for what reason of the desire of their flesh, only God knows, they went their *own way*.

This truth must not be ignored. The more we go our *own way*, the more we forget what we looked like. We become offended when given the truth of the scriptures. We resemble more and more the world. We start camping closer and closer to Sodom (Sin City) until we move in bringing our children with us as did Lot.

Many of us who once looked in the glass and saw our true reflection are now hearers only. We have chosen to go our *own way* and have forgotten what we saw. We have forgotten our sins separate us from God. We have allowed our unfaithful heart to convince our mind we are what we are not. Because of our knowledge, we sit in church and have all the answers. However, we are no longer doers of the word, but have become hearers only deceiving our own selves.

Deception of Hearing Only

We cannot be a doer of the word unless we continue in the perfect Law of Liberty. That means we are **always** looking in the glass, so we do not forget what our natural face, our old nature looks like.

Christianity is not what we believe, but what we do. Yet, the doing must be rooted in belief. The devils believe and tremble, but they will not be saved. Why will they not be saved? Because they do not do what they believe. They are hearers only and have deceived their own selves.

A doer of the word always sees what we really are. Our heart cannot flatter ourselves into thinking our sin is not so bad. Our conscience is held captive to the Word of God. We do not let anything or anyone deter us from the glass which is the Word of God or the Law of Liberty. Thus, we always behold our natural face before us.

We know what we are and do not forget that it is only because of grace we have been delivered from the chains of Satan and sin. Only as we look into the perfect law of liberty will we persevere and keep our bodies under. As doers of the word, we conquer the impediment of being a hearer only of the word and receive an incorruptible crown!

Chapter 5

Fear Subjugates Faith

15)For ye have not received the spirit of bondage again to fear; but ye have received the Spirit of adoption, whereby we cry, Abba, Father. 16)The Spirit itself beareth witness with our spirit, that we are the children of God:17)And if children, then heirs; heirs of God, and joint-heirs with Christ; if so be that we suffer with him, that we may be also glorified together.
(Romans 8:15 – 17)

ALL GOD'S SOLDIERS SHOULD possess a holy fear that is a preventative against negligence in our faith walk. Our fear should be a reverential trust instilling an awe of God's power, holiness, and righteous judgment. A holy fear includes a dread of sinning against him and of the consequences that would follow.

However, the bondage to fear in our scripture text in Romans means to be a slave to; to serve. It denotes being put in fear, alarm, fright, or terror. We are not to be a slave to serve fear, alarm, etc. The children of God have not received the spirit of bondage to fear.

Fear Subjugates Faith

Christ has delivered us from fear's enslavement. We are no longer in bondage or servitude to fear.

God's soldiers must be aware of this stifling fear that will instigate us to doubt the God who spoke all things into existence through his faith. If we permit doubt to take hold of us, we lower God to impotence instead of the God who is omnipotent. Our fear and unbelief produces a God who is powerless.

Has unbelief in the word of God, his promises caused us to see the problem as a giant and our faith in God as a grasshopper? If we continue to believe the lies of doubt, fear will rise up in our heart like a giant. Allowing fear to take hold will find us in the place of the Israelites where faith turns into unbelief. Once our heart becomes discouraged, our confidence in God, in his word, and in his ability will diminish as the walls of our problems ascend.

The fear we have to conquer is the panic that grips us causing us to run away, be alarmed, scared, frightened, dismayed, filled with dread, intimidated, anxious, and apprehensive. Such fear will subjugate faith and disarm us.

It has devastating results. It can virtually paralyze us and make us helpless. Destructive fear stops the flow of God's power. Fear is wrong believing. It is an incorrect perception that will not encourage perseverance in our life.

Dependence on God and a right relationship with him will conquer fear. Without a proper perception of God, fear is an impediment that will control us. Fear is a fleshly response that will subjugate faith.

> *We wrestle not against flesh and blood, but against principalities, against powers, against the rulers of the darkness of this world, against spiritual wickedness in high places. (Ephesians 6:12)*

> *For God hath not given us the spirit of fear; but of power, and of love, and of a sound mind. (2 Timothy 1:7)*

We must recognize the fact that fear is referred to as a **spirit**. It is a spiritual power and force of the enemy to destroy our faith. Fear will cause us to deviate from God's will. We will never face the

Goliaths in our life through fear. In fact, we will lose every battle and be the servant of fear.

That is quite a sobering reality. If fear is ruling our life, we are its servant. Whereas faith liberates us from servitude or bondage to anything. If Jesus has set us free, we are free indeed (John 8:36). We choose whether to be in bondage to the sin of fear or be liberated to trust God.

In 2 Timothy 1:7, Timothy was experiencing great opposition to his message and to himself as a leader. His youth, his association with Paul, and his leadership had come under fire from believers and nonbelievers alike. Paul urged him to be bold. God had not given him a spirit of fear or cowardice.

When we allow people to intimidate us, fear can prevent us from doing God's will. The Israelites revealed in Deuteronomy 1:20 – 33 the negative consequences of listening to the unbelief of people. It is a perfect example of discouragement and its resulting fear that disobeys God.

In those verses, we find the Israelites not entering the Promised Land at their first arrival at Kadesh-Barnea. Although we all know the story of the ten doubting spies giving an evil report and the two faith-filled spies (Joshua and Caleb) giving a righteous report, we need to recognize how fear instigated their response.

> *Whither shall we go up? our brethren have discouraged our heart, saying, The people is greater and taller than we; the cities are great and walled up to heaven; and moreover we have seen the sons of the Anakims there. (Deuteronomy 1:28)*

Here we see the Israelites became discouraged as they concentrated upon the impediments (the walls up to heaven, the giants or Sons of Anakim, and the size of the people) instead of concentrating upon the God whose throne is heaven and the earth is his footstool (Isaiah 66:1).

The word discouraged in the Hebrew means to faint with fear, to melt away; to liquify. According to Merriam-Webster dictionary, fear is dread, fright, alarm, panic, terror, trepidation. It is painful agitation in the presence or anticipation of danger.

Fear Subjugates Faith

They were claiming their brethren had caused them to be without confidence or to have no confidence. Listening to the ten faithless spies caused them to believe they were helpless; thus, they had no hope. Their faith was subjugated by fear.

Are we comprehending who they had no confidence in? This people became full of unbelief. Unbelief yielded a lack of confidence in God and his ability to do as He had promised. Fear overruled faith in the God who had shown himself mighty in Egypt and the miraculous crossing of the Red Sea, etc.

How many times has God told us something and we allow fear to overwhelm our faith? We question whether we have actually heard from God, question if God truly meant for us to do that, question if perhaps we have become too spiritual. Other times, we become weary in the wait that seems to take forever to happen. The time between seedtime and harvest causes us to doubt God will do it.

We can be easily discouraged as we focus on the impediments of the storm, the obstacle, the strategies of Satan day after day, week after week, and year after year. When we allow ourselves to be discouraged during the wait, it is due to a lack of confidence in God. A lack of confidence in God yields a spirit of fear and a loss of hope. We stop persevering, focus on the impediment, and relinquish an incorruptible crown.

The Israelites focused on the evil report of the ten spies and lost sight of the God who had miraculously delivered them from the Egyptian bondage, etc. All they could think about was the walls fortified up to heaven and the giants who made them look like grasshoppers.

How many of God's soldiers are doubting the ability of God to fulfill his promise? How many of us are allowing the impediments of our circumstances, our work, our family, our finances, etc. to appear as if they are unscalable, as if we can never overcome them? How many of us have allowed unbelief in God's word, his promises to cause us to see the problem as a giant and our faith in God as a grasshopper?

Believe me, if we continue to believe the lies of doubt, fear will rise up in our heart. Then we will find ourselves in the place of the Israelites where our faith has turned into unbelief. Our heart will become discouraged, and our confidence and faith in God, his word, his ability will be subjugated, defeated, overcome by fear.

It was fear that caused the Israelites to distrust God. Doubt caused them to believe the God who gave them a mighty deliverance from Egypt, who caused the Red Sea to part and allow them to walk on dry land, could not bring them into the land He promised.

Fear caused them to believe the God who spoke all things into existence had become impotent (powerless) and no longer omnipotent (all-powerful). Almighty God, through their unbelief, had become weak and powerless.

We must be vigilant (persevere) against listening to the doubting Thomas, the arduous journey, the lingering wait, the evil report, etc. that will discourage our heart. We must deny self its affinity to fear that will yield unbelief in God. Unbelief causes us to lose confidence in the only one who can deliver his promise.

> *Fear thou not; for I am with thee: be not dismayed; for I am thy God: I will strengthen thee; yea, I will help thee; yea, I will uphold thee with the right hand of my righteousness. (Isaiah 41:10)*

God's soldiers must comprehend all believers are God's chosen people. We can claim the promises in that verse as our own. We need not fear or be dismayed no matter what we are facing, because God promises to always to be with us (*I am with thee*). God is assuring us of his relationship with us (*I am thy God*). His pledge of strength, help, and victory to conquer all impediments is certain.

Listen to me, the devil knows if he can generate fear, our next step is unbelief. When this occurs, God is prevented from fulfilling his promise to us. Fear will paralyze our faith. Fear will always subjugate faith. Only as we master our tendency to fear and believe God's word, will we be enabled to persevere, conquer the fleshly impediment of fear, and receive an incorruptible crown!

Chapter 6

Perseverance Conquers Weariness

And let us not be weary in well doing: for in due season we shall reap, if we faint not. (Galatians 6:9)

ALTHOUGH WE QUOTE THIS scripture over and over again, how many of us are allowing ourselves to become weary of the arduous journey? How many of us have forgotten our faith walk is a lifelong marathon? How many of us are weary of restricting our flesh what it wants? How many of us are gradually veering onto the broad and wide path that leads to destruction?

What is weary? It is to be drained, exhausted, depleted. When we are weary, we are depleted of the energy or desire to continue. We give up or give into the weakness of our flesh. We take our eyes off an incorruptible crown, the desire to continue running the race is gone, and we resign ourselves to quitting.

> 24)Know ye not that they which run in a race run all, but one receiveth the prize? So run, that ye may obtain. 25) And every man that striveth for the mastery is temperate in all things. Now they do it to obtain a corruptible crown;

> *but we an incorruptible. 26)Therefore so run, not as uncertainly; so fight I, not as one that beateth the air: 27)But I keep under my body, and bring it into subjection: lest that by any means, when I have preached to others, I myself should be a castaway. (1 Corinthians 9:24 – 27)*

The Apostle contrasts the Christian race with the athletic games of his time. The preparation was extremely grueling on the physical body, and the competition was strenuous. Yet only one could win the prize.

Paul is admonishing God's soldiers to *so run that ye may obtain*. We must be as much in earnest to receive our crown (which all may receive) as those which are in earnest to win (which only one can win). Although only one can win, those athletes were *temperate in all things*.

As an athlete who disciplines self to achieve the end results, God's soldiers must live a life of self-discipline and choose to sacrifice our fleshly desires to accomplish the end results. We must willingly take up our heavy cross of self-denial daily

We should be as earnest to attain Heaven and our incorruptible crown that is immortal as men are to win a race or wrestle an opponent for a corruptible prize that will decay. Athletes, to accomplish their goal of winning their contest, must endure years of severe training with severe self-discipline. If we are to conquer this life and receive our crown, we must persistently persevere and practice self-restraint. We must control our body with its lust of the flesh, the lust of the eyes, and the pride of life.

When we think about athletes, we are reminded of the Olympic athletes who are some of the toughest people we know. These people do not just love the sport they compete in, but it is their life. Most of their life is devoted to their goal of winning an Olympic medal.

Many of these athletes spend four to eight years training in a sport before they make an Olympic team or participate in an Olympic competition. They do not take lightly their endeavor and plan training schedules years in advance in order to work towards and accomplish their specific goals.

While their friends may be out socializing, the Olympic athletes are denying their flesh any recreation that could hinder their goal of winning the medal. They make sure they adhere to a strict diet, get the sleep needed, and keep themselves in the right state of mind in order to stay on top of their game.

Once God's soldiers recognize we are spiritual athletes, it should change our outlook on how we live our life. We should be totally transformed in our thinking, our goals, and our life in general. Our focus in life should always be on obtaining an incorruptible crown no matter the suffering on our flesh.

Paul, in the scriptures in 1 Corinthians, is teaching us the world runs to win a corruptible crown that will fade away and rot. Even though the Olympic athletes are aware of this fact, the participants are temperate or self-controlled. They abstain from all that could be a hindrance to their winning the contest or the race. They persevere and train laboriously knowing only one will win the gold.

Do God's soldiers comprehend our race has an eternal crown? Do we realize our spiritual well-being is at risk? Do we understand the importance of abstaining from whatever could hinder our incorruptible crown?

The Apostle Paul understood this reality and kept his body under and brought it into subjection to the will of God. He knew the dangers of becoming disheartened, dispirited, discouraged, depressed by the daily impediments he encountered. He fully comprehended if he did not keep his fleshly appetites under control, he would be disqualified from receiving his crown.

We must never stop being temperate in our desires, restrained in our flesh, and constant in our devotion to God. As God's soldier, we must always be self-restraining. Bridles are put into a horse's mouth to control its direction. We must bridle our wants/desires that are the opposite of God's word. We must practice self-denial daily to run this race.

The rewarding thought is that not only one can receive our crown. But all who persevere and run the race with temperance, that is characterized by moral and spiritual purity, integrity, separation from evil and complete dedication to God, will finish the race and receive an incorruptible crown.

If we realize that once we have chosen to be a soldier of God, we have chosen a life of adversity, we will have our heart prepared for any impediment. We cannot fight our flesh today and decide to compromise tomorrow. Because the soldier is concerned about pleasing his superior officer, he does not entangle himself with the affairs of this life. God's soldiers must not concern ourselves with the affairs of this life but focus on pleasing him who has called us to be a soldier.

The athlete does not practice self-restraint one day and indulge the next. He has one goal and that is to win his prize. He is willing to persevere through any impediment or inconvenience to his flesh that will enable him to run his best race. Once God's soldiers comprehend our crown carries eternal consequences, we will gladly deny self its lust of the flesh, lust of the eyes, and pride of life to receive our incorruptible crown.

In short, athletes must live a strict and regimental life of rules and regulations with no assurance of any prize. Our spiritual race has rules and regulations with the assurance of receiving an incorruptible crown. However, our rules are not binding but liberating. Our race frees us from all bondages that could hinder our overcoming. *If the Son therefore shall make you free, ye shall be free indeed* (John 8:36).

> *Be not deceived: God is not mocked: for whatsoever a man soweth, that shall he also reap. (Galatians 6:7)*

To comprehend how becoming weary in our race can prohibit our conquering or overcoming this life and receiving the prize, let us shed more light on the importance of our race.

The above scripture text warns us to *be not deceived*. We are being warned not to go astray. We are not to allow ourselves to err from the way. Do not be deceived.

In chapter four, we talked about the deception of hearing only. Here, I want to help illuminate that truth.

God declares we are not to be deceived. The deception occurs when we deceive ourselves by allowing self or others to influence our thinking contrary to the truth of scripture.

We become hearers only when we do not do the Word of God because we decide which scriptures to shun, or we have allowed a teacher of itching ears to seduce us with fables (2 Timothy 4:3 – 4) or whatever tickles or is pleasant on our flesh.

In order to conquer this life's temptation to stray away from the Word of God, we must not permit ourselves to wander from the straight path, for God will not be mocked. He will not be ridiculed. He will not be laughed at. He will not be made a fool of.

WHAT GOD SAYS WILL BE DONE.

Whatever seed we plant is what we will reap. The crop we harvest can only be whatever seed we have planted. A farmer does not plant corn if he desires a harvest of wheat.

> *For he that soweth to his flesh shall of the flesh reap corruption; but he that soweth to the Spirit shall of the Spirit reap life everlasting. (Galatians 6:8)*

What is the Apostle saying here? He is stating if we live a bad life (a life that yields to the lust of the flesh, the lust of the eyes, and the pride of life), we will reap corruption or Hell. We will not reap an incorruptible crown.

He is clarifying that as our present life is so will be our eternal life. We cannot sow to our flesh (immorality, idolatry, hatred, strife, jealousy, pride, selfishness, drunkenness, fornication, adultery, stubbornness, pornography, etc.) and expect to inherit the kingdom of God (Heaven) or receive an incorruptible crown.

However, if we sow to the Spirit, all that is sown is under the guidance of the Holy Ghost. As we allow the Holy Spirit to direct and influence our lives, the power of sin is destroyed.

> *He must increase, but I must decrease. (John 3:30)*

This scripture is the secret of not becoming weary during our lifelong marathon. Our race is continuous, without end, until we die. It is not run for one race, but it is constant, endless, ceaseless. We will not conquer self and run the race without endless perseverance.

> *I am crucified with Christ: nevertheless I live; yet not I, but Christ liveth in me: and the life which I now live in the flesh I live by the faith of the Son of God, who loved me, and gave himself for me. (Galatians 2:20)*

How can we have endless perseverance or endurance? If we are to continue, we must give up all rights to self. It must not be us living, but Christ living in us. We must be decreasing and He must be increasing until there is less and less visibility of self.

Jesus must become more prominent and we must become less prominent. He must grow stronger and stronger in us, and we must become weaker and weaker. In other words, our spirit must be strong and our flesh must be weak if we are to conquer the impediments of this life.

> *And thou shalt love the Lord thy God with all thy heart, and with all thy soul, and with all thy mind, and with all thy strength: this is the first commandment. (Mark 12:30)*

We cannot decrease or become less unless our love for God exceeds any love we have for self, anyone, or anything. Only as we allow the Holy Ghost to increase in us, can we be influenced to love God with all our heart, soul, mind, and strength.

If the flesh or self is our influence, we love ourselves more. When self is stronger, we will easily become weary during the impediments of storms, facing obstacles, combatting Satan's strategies, or denying self.

Paul, being aware of this truth, kept his body under and brought it into subjection to the will of God. He knew if he gave into the stress, fatigue, hardship, etc. of the marathon, he would become weary. Giving into weariness would cause him to become a castaway or disqualified and lose his crown.

Let me help us comprehend this all further. We know sowing to the flesh will reap corruption or Hell. Whereas, sowing to the Spirit will reap life everlasting or Heaven.

Perseverance Conquers Weariness

Now, a harvest takes time to grow. A farmer must plough the field, plant the seed, tend his fields, etc. before he can bring in the harvest.

The more evil seed (flesh) we sow, the more fleshly is our life. Of course, the more good seed (Spirit) we sow, the more spiritual is our life. Our harvest or what we are reaping reveals what our life is sowing.

Is our life one of turmoil, anxiety, unhappiness, impatience, complaints, doubts, etc.? It is because we are sowing to our flesh.

Listen up, I am not saying our life will not have trials that could cause us to feel some of its negative effects like turmoil, anxiety, etc. What I am saying is sowing to the Spirit will overrule those emotions. We will have *the peace of God which passeth all understanding* (Philippians 4:7). We will know we *can do all things through Christ which strengtheneth* us (Philippians 4:13). We will know *with God all things are possible* (Matthew 19:26). We will know *that all things work together for good to them that love God, to them who are the called according to his purpose* (Romans 8:28).

If we are sowing to the Spirit, our life will experience peace of mind, trust in God, contentment in all impediments. We will be persevering through the denial of self. Only the flesh will cause us to concentrate upon the storm, whereas the Spirit will cause us to concentrate on God's promise and conquer the impediment interfering with our race.

Sowing to the Spirit will give us an intense desire to please God. Nothing else will matter, but pleasing him who gave himself for us. We will be as the Apostle Paul and be content in whatever impediment (storm, obstacle, strategy, grief, etc.) we may find ourselves (Philippians 4:11). Contentment comes from being in his will.

God's purpose for our life may sometimes include affliction, trials, grief, persecution suffering. But God will bring good out of it all. Ultimately the impediments or the fire is for our glorification, but in this life it may be needed to strengthen our faith, our resolve to please him, and the necessity to conquer all impediments.

As a body builder keeps increasing the pounds of weight he lifts to build up his muscles, we must face weightier impediments, storms, or trials to build up our faith. In my book, *Storms Are Faith's Workout*, I explain the necessity for us to be tried.

Endurance or Perseverance cannot occur without the obstacles necessary to conquer. God will provide the impediments for us to practice perseverance. He knows if our faith is not tested, it will not be strengthened. If our faith is not strengthened, we will not persevere. If we do not persevere, we will not conquer the lifelong impediments that must be overcome if we are to receive an incorruptible crown.

Our receiving an incorruptible crown requires our perseverance or running a lifelong race where there is no place for growing weary.

> *For our light affliction, which is but for a moment, worketh for us a far more exceeding and eternal weight of glory.* (2 Corinthians 4:17)

Do we comprehend our trials, difficulties, our lifelong marathon is light compared to the eternal weight of glory that will belong to those who are faithful to Christ to the end? Because of what Christ has waiting for us who overcome, we must never lose hope or give up our faith (our race) as we face all manner of impediments in this life.

> *And he said unto me, My grace is sufficient for thee: for my strength is made perfect in weakness. Most gladly therefore will I rather glory in my infirmities, that the power of Christ may rest upon me.* (2 Corinthians 12:9)

God promises to give heavenly strength to us who depend on him and call on him for assistance. The greater our weaknesses and difficulties in running our race are, the more grace God will give us to persevere until we accomplish or conquer the impediment.

His promised grace is sufficient for us to overcome each day. I know this to be true, for I ask for his grace each day to get me through whatever He has planned for that day. There have been many difficult days, but his grace gets me through. Granted

Perseverance Conquers Weariness

some days are more arduous and require more perseverance of self-denial, but He always gives the grace needed to conquer the impediment.

We must strive to continue to decrease (become less) and allow Christ to increase (become more). As we do that, his grace is sufficient. Because his grace is sufficient and his strength (supernatural) is made perfect in our weakness, we do not have to become weary. Our incorruptible crown is worth any self-denial or impediment we may have to face in this life!

Chapter 7

Balance the Impediment

28)Come unto me, all ye that labour and are heavy laden, and I will give you rest. 29)Take my yoke upon you and learn of me; for I am meek and lowly in heart: and ye shall find rest unto your souls. 30)For my yoke is easy, and my burden is light. (Matthew 11:28 – 30)

IN THESE VERSES JESUS offers an invitation for rest to us who labor and are heavy laden with the impediments of this life.

Chapter five revealed how fear subjugates faith, and chapter six revealed how only perseverance will conquer weariness. This chapter will bring both truths together. If we comprehend God gives us his grace to overcome our weaknesses, we will not become weary or tire from the arduous race for an incorruptible crown. Through his strength, we are enabled to keep in the race. In this chapter, He wants us to comprehend what we carry will hinder the outcome of our race. If we insist on carrying the full load, we will become weary and quit the race.

Balance the Impediment

God does not want His soldiers distraught and overwhelmed with the impediments of cares, trials, troubles, storms, obstacles, politics, or evils of this world. Our life is to be one that experiences God's strength no matter what is going on in our life, the life of others, the world, the political arena, etc.

Jesus says, *Come unto to me, all ye that labour and are heavy laden.* This implies that we have a great load laid upon us, which we must carry to some place. Each step we take is draining our strength, thereby making the load seem heavier. This is the way of our life. But if we go to Jesus, He promises us rest, that we will be refreshed, and that our load will be eased. This rest comes as we allow him to balance the impediment.

Understand these verses are a universal call. We know God calls everyone to repentance from the burden of sin. Yet, we must comprehend this is a call to us who are God's soldiers or believers in Christ.

It appears God's children are laboring with heavy burdens. Our hearts are so heavy that some of us are depressed, want to yield to the flesh, or just walk out of the race.

Some of us think God does not care what we are going through. Some of us believe God makes life harder for those who desire to serve him. We look around at the lost and they seem to live an easier life. However, we forget, the devil is not bothered about their lives. The ungodly are going to Hell (Psalm 73:17).

We forget the need for the fire of trials, impediments, etc. to have our faith purified. Only pure faith will be found onto praise, and honor, and glory when Jesus returns. It is time for us to quit looking at the obstacles and focus on an incorruptible crown waiting for those who conquer their flesh.

As the world looks in all the wrong places for a cure or help, there are many of God's soldiers doing the same.

How many of us are doing things contrary to the Word of God? How many of us are not truly trusting God, but claiming we are? How many of us are doing things that reveal we do not have full confidence in God? How many of us through sin have left the straight and narrow way and are now travelling the broad and wide way?

The Gospel was purposed to be the remedy for all the miseries, fear, hurt, grief, pain, storms, obstacles, etc. that have entered the world as the result of sin.

Jesus says to the weary heart, *come unto me*. What a blessed comment for the weary in heart to hear. Think about that statement. It is God Almighty reaching out to us who are overloaded and says, *come unto me*. He says for us who are laboring under a heavy load to approach him, and He will give us rest.

How many of us have rest? How many feel the burden or load is heavier? Have we approached Jesus? If we have, why are we claiming the load is just as heavy? If it is just as heavy, we have not approached Jesus and taken his yolk upon us.

How can our load be eased? He says if we take his yoke upon us, we will find rest. His *yoke* is that of faith in him, in his word, in his ability, in his power, in his love, etc. If we can picture a traditional kitchen scale in our minds, that will help us to understand Christ's yoke. His *yoke* in the Greek means to join; the beam of a balance as connecting the scale. It is the beam that joins the pans on either side. One pan has the weights and the other pan has the load or that which is being weighed. Without the weights in the opposite pan, the load would drop.

The impediments of this life could drain our strength and cause us to collapse under the load, but it is balanced when we come to Jesus and take his yoke upon us. How is the load balanced? Verse 29 says, *Take my yoke upon you, and learn of me.* Jesus will teach God's soldiers how He balances the heavy load. Without Jesus, there is no beam to balance our load. Only as we yoke up with Christ is the load balanced and we find rest for our soul. We have to quit trying to carry things in our strength, in our knowledge, in our wisdom, in our education, etc.

The Greek says *rest* means to repose, to be refreshed, to have intermission, to have recreation. Yet, Webster's 1828 dictionary says *rest* is a quiet repose, a state of reconciliation to God, a state free from motion or disturbance.

Balance the Impediment

Jesus tells us to *learn of me*. Now, that is telling us to learn the ways of Jesus or learn from his example. In *Storms Are Faith's Workout*, I used Mark 4:35-40 which shows us what rest in action looks like. The storm in Mark is a whirlwind, a tempest, or a violent storm. Now, a violent storm is definitely a disturbance. Yet, Webster's 1828 tells us the rest Jesus gives us is a state free from disturbance.

Now, Mark 4 informs us while this disturbance, this tempest, this violent storm is raging Jesus slept. Yet, his disciples were in fear, terror, and panic. Think about that. When the tempest comes into our life, are we asleep with Jesus or are we panicking through fear with the disciples?

Let us understand something here. When it says Jesus was asleep, it means Jesus was refreshing himself during a violent storm. He wants God's soldiers to learn from him. We need to learn how to rest or be refreshed no matter what is going on. We are to take recreation during the labor, the heavy loads, the storms, the trials of life, or the impediments. It means the ability to persevere until we conquer the impediment.

Once God's soldiers learn to walk daily dressed in God's full armor, we will do as Jesus did and rest during the storm. If we understand the scale discussed earlier, we will comprehend what Jesus meant by taking his yoke upon us. What Jesus is saying to us is that He wants to be the balancing beam. He wants to be the one that connects the scales, or the one who is the balancer. He desires to stable our load so that we are not overwhelmed by its weight.

If we look at a scale and see the two pans are balanced by the beam. On the left is the load and on the right is the weights. If we do not use the proper weights the load on the left tips the scale. In our life, that means we are overwhelmed, oppressed, worried, fearful, and feel undone. Our strength or our will to go on seems to be gone. We feel completely crushed and without hope.

When this happens, we are like the disciples in the boat and feel we are about to be destroyed. But according to Jesus, we are in this state because of unbelief (Mark 4:40). If we as God's soldiers have been learning from these impediments, we should be asleep with Jesus in the boat. We should be experiencing his rest. We should be denying our flesh its propensity to fear.

If we believe all we have been taught concerning faith in the word of God, we will be asleep, resting, and being refreshed during the storm. We will persevere no matter how severe the impediment being faced. In order to persevere and experience the rest promised by Christ, we must believe God loves us, we must trust his divine plan for our life, and we must trust in his grace that is sufficient for any impediment.

We need to comprehend what rest is like. A baby rests in his mother's arms, contented, and totally trusting in mother to care, to protect, to feed, to love, to comfort, and to meet every need. The baby never thinks about trusting; it comes naturally. The baby expects mommy to do it. That is what Jesus was doing in the boat. His faith in his Father to protect, etc. enabled him to rest in that faith. Because God promised to take them to the other side, Jesus expected him to fulfill his word. We need to follow Christ's example and expect God to fulfill his promise, his word to us.

Now, what impediment are we facing? What storm has us fighting its power? What load is becoming too distressing? Is it our children, our job, our finances, a sickness, grief, an evil report? Whatever it is, Jesus said He will balance it. His yoke is easy, and his burden is light.

Think about the scale again. The storm (whatever it may be) is on the left. Jesus is the beam balancing the two pans. Now, what does He use as the weight on the right to balance the load? It is quite simple, Jesus uses the word of God. Our knowledge of the word enables us to use whatever weight (promise, etc.) needed for Jesus to balance the load enabling us to live in a constant rest during whatever impediment is attempting to thwart our race.

This is an important factor God's soldiers must comprehend. If we are using man's knowledge, man's wisdom, man's science, man's logic, man's medicine, etc. then our faith is in them. Our weight during any storm must be God's word. Only His word can balance the scale or the burden we are carrying.

Balance the Impediment

Jesus Christ the same yesterday, and to day, and forever.
(Hebrews 13:8)

The fact Jesus never changes is an anchor for our life and faith. If Jesus promised rest to us who are under heavy burdens 2,000 years ago, that promise holds true today. We serve a God who cannot lie (Titus 1:2).

If we come to Jesus with our heavy load of trouble or misery and come away without rest or ease from our heavy burden, then we have not truly approached God in faith. We have not taken on his yoke.

Let me give an example how fear tries to overrule a word from the Lord. My husband became blind in his right eye and legally blind in his left eye from cataracts. Apparently he was blind in his right eye for about two years or more, and legally blind in his left eye. Due to a financial situation, he did not let me know how severe his eyesight was.

I was told by the Lord to make an appointment for him with an optometrist. When I called, there was an appointment available in a month. I asked if there was something sooner. The receptionist asked me to wait, and said there was a cancellation that day. We had an hour to get there. That is when we discovered the cataracts and the severity of his eyesight.

The optometrist recommended an ophthalmologist. When I called them, we were told we had a two month wait. I again asked if something was available sooner. The receptionist asked me to wait and said a cancellation had been made for the following day.

Anyway, we did not have the resources to have the expensive laser surgery with the special lenses. I prayed and the Lord reminded me of someone who was blind and had a glass eye and could see out of the glass eye. He told me to trust him, have the surgery, and the artificial lens would work as Paul's natural lens.

For three days after the surgery on his right eye, he could see only light and vague dark shadows without making out what they were. He was set up to have the left eye done in three weeks. We were both feeling anxious about surgery in the left eye when he could not see out of the right. That would mean he would be totally blind. It was only his left eye that he had been able to see out of for a couple of years. Fear was trying to cause us to join the disciples in the boat.

I sought the Lord with what I believed He promised me. I prayed for grace to conquer the fear trying to rise up in me and Paul. I quoted *for God hath not given us a spirit of fear, but of power, and of love, and of a sound mind*. I quoted *for with God all things are possible*. During the prayer, the Lord reassured me, He is not a man that He can lie. I had yoked up with Jesus during this impediment and sensed the peace of God that passes all understanding.

He then revealed Paul would start seeing out of his right over the weekend. After another week, he was seeing 20/60 out of his right eye. Then the weekend before surgery on his left eye, he could see the back yard with his right eye and was ecstatic to see colors. He had surgery on his left eye on a Tuesday. When he was examined the day after surgery, he had 20/20 vision in his right eye and 20/40 already in his left eye.

Now, please understand there have been times when conquering the impediment took weeks and weeks, months and months, and sometimes years of perseverance before things changed. Some things have yet to change, but I hang onto God's promise. As long as I yoke up with Christ, I receive the rest needed to persevere each day. Anytime I become overwhelmed by the impediment, I feel the turmoil of the disciples in the ship. If I feel myself becoming crushed by the impediment and joining the disciples in their frenzy, I immediately **quote the word** and believe God to give me rest. At that, Jesus balances the load or impediment, and I join him asleep in the boat.

He always gives me the rest I need to persevere another a day. I believe we need to understand our conquering impediments is a **daily** task. If we are to persevere, we must take up our cross of self-denial daily. We do not conquer without perseverance. We do not receive the perseverance required to conquer daily impediments without yoking up with Christ.

Balance the Impediment

Christ desires to bring rest to our troubled souls more than we desire it. He did not suffer the cross for us to be defeated by sin through the impediments or storms of this life.

Rest and peace can only come if we bring the load to him in faith. We must believe him to balance the load through his word and give us his promised rest. However, if we insist on carrying it ourselves and ignore his word, He cannot be our balancing beam.

If our load is unbearable or heavy, shame on us. We have refused to allow him to balance the weight with his word. Unbelief or doubt has caused the other pan to be empty of God's word or promises. Filling it with self, doubt, unbelief, etc. will make our load heavier and heavier.

We must ask ourselves if our burden has become too heavy. Are we carrying the full load and impeding our race instead of allowing Jesus to balance it? Are we questioning if this is really worth it? Are we contemplating quitting the race because self-denial is too burdensome? Are we living for Christ and an incorruptible crown or are we living for this life and its corruptible prize?

> *For I reckon that the sufferings of this present time are not worthy to be compared with the glory which shall be revealed in us. (Romans 8:18)*

Eternity should be our focus and not this life. As we consider Christ's sacrifice and his offer to balance the impediment for us to conquer this life, all selfish thoughts disappear. We constantly approach Jesus with our burdens and allow him to balance the scale through faith in his word. Whatever hardship we suffer in this life cannot be compared with the glory of receiving an incorruptible crown awaiting all who persevere and conquer all impediments!

Chapter 8

Follow the Directions

Enter ye in at the strait gate: for wide is the gate, and broad is the way, that leadeth to destruction, and many there be which go in thereat: Because strait is the gate, and narrow is the way, which leadeth unto life, and few there be that find it. (Matthew 7:13 – 14)

GOD'S SOLDIERS HAVE THE choice as to which direction we will follow. There are two ways or paths, but only one direction is his way.

The entrance into the strait gate or Heaven is restricted. Only those willing to do the will of God may enter there at. Whereas the entrance into the wide gate or Hell is unrestricted. If we are not willing to face hardships, persecution, storms, etc. to overcome this life, we will choose to follow the wide and broad path.

Choosing the straight and narrow means we will endeavor to face whatever obstacles may occur in this life. Our mindset is on persevering and conquering all impediments because our heart is

Follow the Directions

not attached to this life but to eternal life. We have set our attention on receiving an incorruptible crown.

> 22)But Jesus answered and said, Ye know not what ye ask. Are ye able to drink of the cup that I shall drink of, and to be baptized with. . . 23)And he saith unto them, Ye shall drink indeed of my cup, and be baptized with the baptism that I am baptized with. (Matthew 20:22 – 23)

Too many believe because Jesus died for our sins, we are to glide through this life without any struggles. Yet, Jesus makes clear to follow him means being partaker of his cup. The cup of suffering for Christ was his death on the cross.

> 12)Beloved, think it not strange concerning the fiery trial which is to try you, as though some strange thing happened unto you: 13)But rejoice, inasmuch as ye are partakers of Christ's sufferings; that, when his glory shall be revealed, ye may be glad also with exceeding joy. (1 Peter 4:12 – 13)

If we are to follow Jesus, we must comprehend it means the need for suffering in our flesh, it means taking up our heavy cross of self-denial daily. Jesus chose to drink the cup of suffering God had planned for him. He knew the agony his flesh would suffer, but he did not look at the suffering for a season. He was focused upon the prize of us, God's soldiers, who are now part of the family of God.

We, alone, choose to drink the cup God has planned for our life. No matter how severe we think our present sufferings are, we must realize our cup will pale in comparison to the cup required of Christ.

Now, if we are to drink our cup of suffering, we must learn to follow the directions. This life will encounter many temptations to avoid the cup. Our flesh will be tempted to meander onto the wide and broad way without the restrictions on our flesh.

> And he said to them all, If any man will come after me, let him deny himself, and take up his cross daily, and follow me. (Luke 9:23)

Only following his directions of denying our flesh daily will keep us on the straight and narrow way. Jesus followed the directions of denying himself and willingly went to the cross which was the ultimate self-denial.

We need to understand about temptations and the necessity of following the directions of God's word.

> *There hath no temptation taken you but such as is common to man: but God is faithful, who will not suffer you to be tempted above ye are able; but will with the temptation also make a way of escape, that ye may be able to bear it.* (1 Corinthians 10:13)

God's soldiers have no alibi for not following God's directions during any temptation. We can never justify our actions with paltry excuses we are human, we did not mean it, it was his or her fault. Besides, I am not perfect like Christ.

Temptations are impediments of trials or storms with a beneficial purpose and effect. They are necessary components to teach us how to deny self, run the race set before us, and receive an incorruptible crown.

Although we may be tempted, there is no sin in the temptation. The sin occurs when we yield to the temptation and sin against God's directions or the Word of God.

To continue, I am going to repeat some thoughts I previously stated in another book explaining temptation. Through that, it will reveal the importance of following the directions.

According to the Greek, temptation means a putting to proof (by experiment of good or of evil; solicitation, entice). An understanding of 1 Corinthians 10:13 will determine victory or defeat during the time of temptation. The devil is the tempter (Matthew 4:3–11) and he is relentless in his plan of seduction to lure us away from the truth of the Scriptures or following the directions. He is so bold that he tried to tempt Jesus. However, Christ knew the directions, because He was not only knowledgeable in the word, but He knew how to rightly divide it. Jesus stayed clothed in the full armor of God and was proficient with the sword of the Spirit which is the word of God.

Follow the Directions

God's soldiers must understand we do not have to fall prey to temptation. If we are enticed by the deceitfulness of sin, we could find ourselves on the wide and broad way.

In the numbered list below is revealed the main points in 1 Corinthians 10:13.

1. What is true about every temptation we face?

    a. They are common to all men.
    b. There is no new type of temptation.
    c. None of us have a monopoly on any certain temptation.
    d. We are not the first to be tempted with the enticement.

2. Who can give us victory when we are tempted?

    a. It is God who is faithful to make a way or the direction to follow.

3. Does He promise to remove the temptation?

    a. No, He does not.

4. What does God actually promise to do?

    a. He promises to make a way of escape, an escape route, the directions to take enabling us to bear the temptation and not be overcome by it.

As we travel along faith's journey, we will face many impediments or temptations with numerous crossroads and intersections. Satan is the tempter who is always trying to get us to avoid the directions and make a wrong turn. The devil continuously tries to seduce, entice, or lure us into sin. Now, we know Satan is the tempter, but what is the major source of temptation?

> 13)*Let no man say when he is tempted, I am tempted of God: for God cannot be tempted with evil, neither tempteth he any man:* 14)*But every man is tempted, when he is drawn away of his own lust, and enticed. (James 1:13 – 14)*

This verse makes clear it is our own lusts that cause us to give into temptation. We are tempted because of the lust of the flesh, the lust of the eyes, and the pride of life instilled in our old nature. If we refuse to take up our heavy cross of self-denial daily, our old nature will resurrect at the drop of a hat. Our old nature revels in all things opposite of following God's directions.

If we do not comprehend the dangers of ignoring the Word of God, we will not deny self to persevere and conquer the temptations or impediments in this life.

The story of the Fall in Genesis describes human temptation does not come from God, but Satan. Adam and Eve's temptation forced them to decide for or against God.

When the devil appears in Job chapter one, temptation is allowed by God as a test. Job meets the test because, even in incomprehensible suffering, he is ready to trust God and commit himself to him. Yes, when Job was attacked physically, he began to accuse God of being unjust. But when God appeared, Job saw the error of his way and repented (Job 42).

The main point of all impediments is that due to the evil impulses or (that which is common to man) testing always means the temptation to take the wrong turn or ignore the directions. Each impediment, temptation, or test has the end result of pass (succeed) or fail (flunk).

In Judges 2:22, God tested the people by not driving out the heathen who still inhabited the land. Would they obey God and drive out the heathen, or would they succumb to the idolatrous worship around them, their own desires, etc.

No matter what the impediment to be conquered, God always provides a way of escape. He continuously gives the necessary directions to follow. Our degree of consecration to God will determine the choice we make. Will we gratify the lust of the flesh, the lust of the eyes, and the pride of life, or will we deny self its lusts?

God's soldiers must realize the impediments of temptations, storms, obstacles, strategies of Satan are the lot of every one of us or we will not conquer them. We are on trial or face impediments our whole life on this earth. It is our choice here that determines our next abode. We are in the race to receive an incorruptible crown. Comprehending the need for temptations, trials, impediments, encourages us to keep running until we have finished our race.

If we think we are going to live this life and be separate or free from impediments, temptations, or tests, we are in for a rude awakening. God's word makes clear only those who overcome will inherit all things; and God will be his God, and he shall be God's son (Revelation 21:7). Again, we are encouraged to keep following the direction of denying self to conquer and receive an incorruptible crown. However, it also reveals the impediments to test our self-denial, are to teach us to overcome.

> 15)And that from a child thou hast known the holy scriptures, which are able to make thee wise unto salvation through faith which is in Christ Jesus. 16)All scripture is given by inspiration of God, and is profitable for doctrine, for reproof, for correction, for instruction in righteousness: 17)That the man of God may be perfect, thoroughly furnished unto all good works. (2 Timothy 3:15 – 17)

It is the Word of God that makes us wise. It will teach us the love and the will of God. It is the active usage of the word (following the directions) without waiver which causes our faith to remain strong during all temptations. As our faith strengthens, we are enabled to persevere and conquer all impediments.

If the early Church did not know the promises of God or the Word of God, they could never have persevered or endured such persecutions. Think about what impediments or self-denial they had to conquer (the arena, burning at the stake, torn by wild animals, etc.) and yet they finished victoriously their race and received their incorruptible crown.

I believe American Christians have become too soft. Let us be truthful. We get crushed if someone calls us a name. How many think the world has caved in because we lost a game or our team lost a game? Yet, when does a team losing a game or our losing a game have anything to do with eternity? Why are we so foolish? It is because we are building our house on the sand and not the rock. We are living for this life and not the next.

Now then we are ambassadors for Christ. (2 Corinthians 5:20)

Dearly beloved, I beseech you as strangers and pilgrims, abstain from fleshly lusts, which war against the soul. (1 Peter 2:11)

Comprehending we are ambassadors for Christ will enable us to realize this is not our home. We are strangers and pilgrims passing through to our country.

It is like a country's ambassador to some country. He lives in the other country, but it is not his home. We live here on earth, but it is not our home. Our home is Heaven whose builder and maker is God (Hebrews 11:10). With that revelation, we are encouraged to follow the directions to our home.

I have heard some Christians say they wish God would take away all evil influences, temptations, etc. However, God has made clear in his word the impediments of temptations, trials, storms are needed if we are going to overcome in this life. That is why God did not drive out the Heathen from the Promise Land (Judges 2:22), and why the wheat and tares grow up together (Matthew 13:24 – 30).

They are here to be stumbling blocks to those who do not choose to follow the directions of denying self. It is our responsibility to study and know the Word of God which is our road map of what direction to take.

At this time, I will interject my favorite example of a temptation. We have diabetes and we ask God to bless this big piece of chocolate cake to our body. We know our physician made clear we are not to have it. We ignore the directions of denying self and eat it. Or course, our sugar level is out of control. We sinned, because we knew better than to abuse our body, but chose not to do it (James 4:17).

The point of this is we are drawn away into sin by our own lusts. Whenever we are tempted and yield to the lust of the flesh, the lust of the eyes, and the pride of life, we fall prey to the enemy. If we do well, sin will desire us, but we will rule over it. If we do not

Follow the Directions

do well, sin is lying at the door, and it will overcome us (Genesis 4:7). This is temptation in a nutshell. We either choose to do well and rule over the temptation to sin, or we choose to yield to our owns lusts and allow sin to overcome us.

Any time we say, "God, I cannot take this anymore," or "this is more than I am able to bear," we have called God a liar. It is doing what the devil said Job would do. We are literally cursing God to his face. Listen to me, God says our impediment or trial is common to all men, and that He has promised a way of escape, a way to persevere and endure, or the direction out.

Our way of escape or way to persevere is his love and his word. It is hanging on and not letting go. How do you think the Christians in my book, *Satan's Strategy to Torment Through Physical Ambush* were enabled to endure such persecution? It was not their own strength. We can only persevere or endure as we trust in the love of God and love him with our very life. Those early Christians knew, according to his word, what they were about to endure was for a moment. That was their way out, their direction to follow. For when it was over, they would be in glory with their Savior (2 Corinthians 4:17).

> *And thine ears shall hear a word behind thee, saying, This is the way, walk ye in it, when ye turn to the right hand, and when ye turn to the left. (Isaiah 30:21)*

> *Thus saith the Lord, Stand ye in the ways, and see, and ask for the old paths, where is the good way, and walk therein, and ye shall find rest for your souls. (Jeremiah 6:16)*

It is time to comprehend no impediment or temptation can overtake us without our choice. Every temptation comes before the moment of decision. What does that mean? If we are driving down the road and we come to an intersection, we choose what direction to take. As we run our race, we will come to a crossroad of temptation or the way out, the Holy Spirit will prompt our heart which road to take. He will always give the proper direction to avoid the temptation.

The above scripture in Isaiah reveals what way we are to walk in, what direction to take. Whereas Jeremiah is urging us to take the old paths. God's people had strayed from God and his plan for their lives. Here He was calling them back to the straight and narrow path that leads to him.

No matter what impediment, the old path, the straight and narrow path is always the proper direction to take. It is following the Word of God without deviating from the path.

All born again believers are promised the Holy Spirit will guide us into all truth (John 16:13). That means no matter the impediment or temptation, the Holy Spirit will cause a hesitation through the word of God (we will hear a voice behind us telling us what direction to follow). None of us claiming to be a Christian goes right into a temptation unless we have ignored the warning, listened to the deceitfulness of sin, yielded to the desire of our flesh, and went in the direction of the flesh.

Let me give some examples of a crossroad by listing some temptations and the way of escape:

1. **Temptation:** Evil thoughts.

    Escape Direction: Let the words of my mouth, and the meditation of my heart, be acceptable in thy sight, O Lord, my strength, and my redeemer (Psalm 19:14).

2. **Temptation:** Too tired to go to Church.

    Escape Direction: Not forsaking the assembling of ourselves together, as the manner of some is; but exhorting one another: and so much the more, as ye see the day approaching (Hebrews 10:25).

3. **Temptation:** To tell a lie or sow discord among the brethren.

    Escape Direction: The Lord hates a lying tongue and sowing discord among the brethren is an abomination to the Lord (Proverbs 6:16–19).

4. **Temptation:** Date or go into business with a non-believer.

Escape Direction: Be ye not unequally yoked together with unbelievers (2 Corinthians 6:14–18).

5. **Temptation:** Murmuring and complaining.

   Escape Direction: Do all things without murmurings and disputings (Philippians 2:14).

Satan has tempted us with the temptation. The impediment is before us. However, the Holy Spirit has quickened with the way of escape or the direction to take. That is when the devil will further tempt us with lies about the Lord. He will imply we are too weak to overcome this obstacle. Yet, the Lord promises we can do all things through Christ which strengtheneth us (Philippians 4:13). He will insinuate God expects too much from us. Yet God promises we are never tempted with more than what we can handle (1 Corinthians 10:13).

God will not remove the temptation. It is up to us to make the right decision and follow his directions. It is time for God's soldiers to quit blaming him for the messes in our life. We must choose to avoid whatever could tempt us into sin. It is imperative for us to realize there are certain situations where we could give place to the devil. For instance, if we had a problem with pornography, why are we at the beach, etc.? If we had overcome alcoholism, why are we at that drunken party? If we had a problem with drugs, why are we around those who are addicted? Some of us have been completely delivered, but others are still battling the temptation to go back. Wisdom is justified of her children (Luke 7:35). God will **never** direct us to be where temptation could overcome us.

Let me make something clear here. All impediments we face are like intersections. We are the ones who decide which direction we take. Do you remember when vehicles did not have power steering? Well, when we are at the moment of decision, we must turn ourselves like we did the vehicle in the direction to go. Sometimes turning the truck was quite a challenge. That is the way it is at times for us. Fighting our flesh to persevere and conquer the impediment can be quite exhausting, but it must be done if we are going to receive our incorruptible crown.

We cannot stay forever at an intersection or crossroad. The tempter has tempted us, and the Holy Spirit has given us the word that is our escape route. Now, we are at the moment of decision. The devil cannot make us do anything against our will, and the Holy Spirit will not make us do anything against our will. It is our decision which way we go. Which direction will we take? Whether we love God more than self will determine which voice we listen to, and what direction we take.

As we continue on our race, it is not a matter of all roads meet in the end. There is only one way to get to where we are heading. The straight and narrow way that leads to life will be extremely difficult on our flesh. Whereas the wide and broad way that leads to destruction is extremely agreeable on our flesh with its lusts and appetites (Matthew 7:13–14). One road is living a life of self-denial of all that is unrighteous and the other road is a life of self-indulgence of all that is unrighteous.

If we are driving someplace and we do not follow the directions, we will not end up at our destination. That same principle must be followed at the time of temptation. Only as we follow the straight and narrow that constricts our flesh will we end up in Heaven. Following the broad and wide indulging our flesh will lead us to Hell. There is no middle road. It is either one or the other. Flesh will choose the broad and wide that leads to destruction. Spirit will choose the straight and narrow that leads to life.

This reveals it takes an effort on our part. We must initiate the resistance against the temptation. If we crucify our flesh and its lusts, God will help us to succeed. He cannot resist for us. It is our free will that decides what we do. We can be assured if we fight and wrestle our fleshly desires and yield to the Holy Spirit, He will show the way of escape or the direction to take. Following God's directions will enable us to persevere, conquer all impediments, and receive an incorruptible crown!

Chapter 9

The War Within

11)Likewise reckon ye also yourselves to be dead indeed unto sin, but alive unto God Through Jesus Christ our Lord. 12)Let not sin therefore reign in your mortal body, that ye should obey it in the lusts thereof. 13)Neither yield ye your members as instruments of unrighteousness unto sin: but yield yourselves unto God, as those that are alive from the dead, and your members as instruments of righteousness unto God. 14)For sin shall not have dominion over you: for ye are not under the law, but under grace. 15)What then: shall we sin, because we are not under the law, but under grace? God forbid. 16)Know ye not, that to whom ye yield yourselves servants to obey, his servants ye are to whom ye obey; whether of sin unto death, or of obedience unto righteousness? 23)For the wages of sin is death; but the gift of God is eternal life through Jesus Christ our Lord. (Romans 6:11 – 16, 23)

An Incorruptible Crown

> *For the flesh lusteth against the Spirit, and the Spirit against the flesh: and these are contrary the one to the other; so that ye cannot do the things that ye would.*
> *(Galatians 5:17)*

CONQUERING OUR OLD NATURE or our flesh is a spiritual conflict we must persevere or endure our whole life. The war within involves our mind, spirit, and body. It is a battle raging within to test whether we will give in to our own sinful desires and give sin control of our life; or will we yield to the Holy Ghost and allow Christ to have authority and control of our life.

This war can never be overcome unless we comprehend when we became born again, we died to sin and self. Because we have received Christ's power to resist sin, we are to live a new life of obedience to God.

Since sin no longer has rule over us, we are to live a life continually resisting sin and its power. Our body is our weak point and sin is ever endeavoring to arouse the desires of our flesh. We must resist the temptation by relying on the spiritual strength available through Christ. He has set us free from the bondage of sin, from its shackles, from its control (John 8:36).

> 2)*Grace and peace be multiplied unto you through the knowledge of God, and of Jesus our Lord,* 3)*According as his divine power hath given unto us all things that pertain unto life, and godliness, through the knowledge of him that hath called us to glory and virtue:* 4)*Whereby are given unto us exceeding great and precious promises: that by these ye might be partakers of the divine nature, having escaped the corruption that is in the world through lust.*
> *(2 Peter 1:2 – 4)*

In the previous chapter, it was revealed the necessity to follow the directions. Here, we must see the war within that rages and how vital a knowledge of God and his word is to following his directions.

The more knowledge of the word, the more we know what direction to take. We cannot conquer the war within without knowing the strategy to win or the way out of the temptation. Only the Word of God will give us the correct direction to pursue.

God has given us all things pertaining unto life and godliness through the knowledge of him. Because we have been given great and precious promises in his word, we become partakers of the divine nature and escape the corruption that is in the world through lust.

As our spirit grows in knowledge of him and his word, we become more and more like Jesus (partakers of the divine nature). The more like him we become, the more power we have to escape the corruption in the world. We have the means to persevere, conquer all impediments, and receive an incorruptible crown.

The power of sin has been severed in our lives once we become born again. To sin now is a choice to do so. Sin has no power over us. It cannot force us to yield to its power. Christ has given us power or authority over all the power of Satan (Luke 10:19).

Wrestling with our old nature can be cumbersome if we are not rooted in the knowledge of God. It is the Word of God that is our way out of any impediment, temptation, storm, obstacle, or strategy of Satan.

The verses in Romans chapter six, set before us the choice of two lives. One is living our life in the old sinful nature of the flesh, and the other is living our life in the new nature of the Spirit.

We must **daily** choose which life we will live. This reveals our life is a constant life of opposition or continuous war. As soldiers at war must always be alert to the enemy and his strategies, that is our daily task. If the enemy can get an advantage, sin will overcome us and take us captive.

There are only two choices or two directions in this life. We choose our service or who reigns in our life. We either serve God or we serve sin. There is no other option.

Let me clarify some points. In Romans 6:12, we find the word REIGN and in verse fourteen, we find the word DOMINION. Both words refer to sin.

As we look at the Greek, both words reveal their meaning stems from lordship. The concept of lordship combines the two elements of power and authority. It is saying if something reigns or has dominion, it is **lord**. It is who or what we serve and give our fidelity to.

In verse sixteen, we find the word SERVANTS. The Greek means to serve or to be under service of. We are either servants or slaves to sin or to God. Who we serve determines our success or failure in persevering and conquering the impediments of this life.

Sin is a very exacting tyrant. It is merciless. As a matter of fact, when we become the slaves or servants of sin, we cease being our own master. When that occurs, we are no longer in control, and sin steers our life. We are not the master of our life, sin is. Sin has become our lord, because it has dominion over us. Sin rules us, we do not rule it. We cannot partake of sin and believe we can stop at any time. It grabs hold of us and imprisons us in its grasp until it reigns or rules our life. We are imprisoned in chains that seem unbreakable.

When sin reigns, we lose the dignity of our nature. We lose self-command. We lose will-power. Our bodies become the instruments of unrighteousness and the lust of the flesh are obeyed.

Sin is not only a tyrant beating us into subjection, but it is a poor paymaster. Romans 6:23 discloses it pays spiritual death. Not an acceptable wage, is it? Yet how many have accepted its wage because of the lust of the flesh, the lust of the eyes, and the pride of life?

Even those who believe sin has pleasure to offer find out it was only for a season. Many in Hell will find out too late their wages of sin is their final wage.

God's soldiers must be honest with ourselves, even in this life, what does sin bring after a while? Does it ever satisfy? I mean, does it bring total fulfillment or the desire for more and more until there is agony, shame, remorse, and a horrible tempest?

Look at those enslaved by gambling, drugs, alcohol, pornography, fornication, greed, fame, etc., they are on a continuous downward spiral into misery that shackles their mind, body, and spirit in unbreakable chains.

> 20)But the wicked are like the troubled sea, when it cannot rest, whose waters cast up mire and dirt. 21)There is no peace, saith my God, to the wicked. (Isaiah 57:20 - 21)

God promises the wicked, those shackled in sin will never have any peace. Their life will be one of unrest. It will be like the troubled sea that cannot rest. They will constantly bring up mire and dirt. The longer in the shackles of sin, the more the torment is seen in their lives. Such anguish cannot be hid. It is as visible as the troubled sea casting up mire and dirt.

Besides the lack of rest, peace, or satisfaction, sin in our lives separates us from God. Continuation in sin brings the wages of death which is separation from God forever.

Now, once we are delivered through being born again or being reconciled with God through the acceptance of Christ, we go from slavery to sin to becoming servants of God. Once freed from sin, we are at liberty to serve God and choose to be his slave or servant. However, this slavery is different.

> I beseech you therefore, brethren, by the mercies of God, that ye present your bodies a living sacrifice, holy, acceptable unto God, which is your reasonable service. (Romans 12:1)

It is a delight, for this slavery is by choice and not by force. God does not imprison us and make us serve him. This yielding or presenting ourselves is without any force or pressure. We see it as a service pleasing to God. Plus, the remarkable result is the pleasure, peace, etc. it brings to us as we resist sin and rest in the presence of God.

In the Old Testament, people brought their sacrifice to the altar of God. The offering was the cream of the crop or the best of the flock. This was given as an atonement for sins. In the above scripture, we are exhorted to offer ourselves in the spirit of sacrifice. We are to be wholly the Lord's property. Unless we comprehend we no longer belong to self but to Jesus, we will never willingly offer ourselves as a living sacrifice.

As a living sacrifice, we choose to follow God's directions for our life. We choose to deny self whatever it may desire. We choose to take up our heavy cross of self-denial daily to persevere, and conquer the impediments of the lust of the flesh, the lust of the eyes, and the pride of life.

> *And he said to them all, If any man will come after me, let him deny himself, and take up his cross daily, and follow me. (Luke 9:23)*

Choosing to follow Christ is not an easy path on the flesh, the old nature, the sinful nature. We may find denying self this or that not too burdensome, but at times denying self this or that is too much on our fleshly desires.

When Christ took up his cross, it meant a brutal means of execution. It represented shame and humiliation. How many of us are willing to identify with Christ and his suffering? How many of us willingly suffer persecution and mockery to be named as his? How many of us willingly choose to live for him and not self?

Choosing to deny self and take up our cross daily is cumbersome. Daily carrying the cross of self-denial can be a difficult task especially as the cross becomes heavier and heavier each day and the pleasures of sin become more and more desirable each day.

Unless we willingly choose to offer our lives as a living sacrifice, we will never be enabled to carry the cross required to conquer and overcome this life. An incorruptible crown will not be obtained by saying a sinner's prayer and then living for self. This crown can only be received through self-denial, offering self as a living sacrifice, and refusing to be the servant of sin.

To persevere against sin and conquer it in our life, we must choose to be his servant and not the servant of sin. With that choice comes the revelation of what an excellent paymaster He is. We comprehend we do not deserve the least of his mercies and that our sins have earned Hell.

We not only grasp the truth we do not deserve any of his blessings, but we also know we are unprofitable servants doing what is our duty (Luke 17:10). We realize the cost of our salvation and that we can never pay for it. Even if we do everything right and never do anything wrong, we have done nothing to pay for our salvation. It is like owing a $1,000,000.00 and we pay $1,000.00. We have not come close to paying our debt, nor can we ever do so, no matter how much right we think we do.

Let us comprehend the difference between Law and Grace. Because sin dominated under the Law, there was no strength in the Law over sin's power. The Law showed sin's ugliness, evil, foulness. It was a monster staring us in the face without any power to defeat it.

The Law revealed the existence and exceeding sinfulness of sin, but it gave no power to resist it. Under the Law, sin kept us in bondage to its control. We recognized the awfulness of it, but was powerless under the Law to be freed from its shackles. The Law condemned sin, but it did not give the way out.

Now, Grace sets us free from the bondage, the lordship, the control, the rulership of sin and death. What I am saying is that GRACE gives us the power over the sin revealed by the Law.

If it were not for the Law, we would not recognize sin. We could know sin was reigning or controlling our life, but the Law could not show us the direction to conquer the evil we saw in our life. It was our schoolmaster teaching us what sin was. It brought us to Christ that we might be justified by faith (Galatians 3:24).

As Grace abounds in our life, sin is unable to lord it over us. It has no power to shackle us in its prison. God's soldiers are the recipients of Grace. We are no longer under the regime of the Mosaic Law as the means of attaining salvation.

Let me clarify what I mean. I do not know how many times I have given the Word of God to those in bondage to sin and been told arrogantly, "We are under Grace, we are not under the Law." They are under the illusion that sin does not matter once they accept Christ. They trod under foot Christ, count his blood an unholy thing, and do despite unto the Spirit of Grace (Hebrews 10:29).

The sad truth is that after I have given them the way out or the directions to follow, they chose to remain shackled in their sin. Through their free-will, they have chosen to alienate themselves from a relationship with Christ.

It grieves my spirit at the ignorance of many of those claiming to be God's soldiers. Because of their chosen ignorance, they are destroyed by a lack of knowledge (Hosea 4:6).

What Romans 6:14 is saying is the opposite of their interpretation. The Apostle Paul is speaking of the reign of sin (those living under the Law) versus the reign of Grace (those living under Grace).

In Romans 6:12, Paul told them to *let not sin therefore reign in your mortal body.* This is telling us that we must not allow sin to rule or have authority and power over us.

Romans 6:14 says, *for sin shall not have dominion over you: for ye are not under the Law, but under Grace.* Sin is not our lord to rule over us now that Grace has come.

Why does sin not have dominion over us? Because we are not under the Law, but under Grace.

> *If the Son therefore shall make your free, ye shall be free indeed. (John 8:36)*

If we are Christ's, we are no longer the servants of sin. Christ made us free from the shackles, the bondage, the control of sin.

This does not mean we are free from the war within us to choose God's direction or follow the lust of our flesh, it means we have been given the power to conquer the sin trying to shackle us. There is no way we can be Christ's and be held captive by sin without willingly yielding our members as instruments of unrighteousness.

Because we have been given much, God requires more of us. Through Grace, we can be master over self, over our sinful nature, over our fleshly appetites. We can always choose the way out and follow the directions of God's word.

We do not serve God because of any chains, or imprisonment, but because we have **chosen** to be his servant in gratitude for his love, mercy, and grace towards us. We have chosen to conquer sin through persevering or enduring until we receive an incorruptible crown at the end of our race!

Chapter 10

A New Horizon

8)By faith Abraham, when he was called to go out into a place which he should after receive for an inheritance, obeyed; and he went out, not knowing whither he went. 9)By faith he sojourned in the land of promise, as in a strange country, dwelling in tabernacles with Isaac and Jacob, the heirs with him of the same promise: 10)For he looked for a city which hath foundations, whose builder and maker is God. 13)These all died in faith, not having received the promises, but having seen them afar off, and were persuaded of them, and embraced them, and confessed that they were strangers and pilgrims on the earth. 14)For they that say such things declare plainly that they seek a country. 15)And truly, if they had been mindful of that country from whence they came out, they might have had opportunity to have returned. 16) But now they desire a better country, that is, an heavenly: wherefore God is not ashamed to be called their God: for he hath prepared for them a city. (Hebrews 11:8 – 10; 13 – 16)

A New Horizon

THIS CHAPTER IS MEANT to help us understand an incorruptible crown is only received if we focus on a new horizon. Our life must have a new perspective contrary to the one we focused upon before we were born again.

In the above verses, we see Abraham did not consider his earthly promise land his final inheritance. He knew he was a sojourner or a foreigner here. His final abode was a city prepared by God to all who conquer the impediments (storms, obstacles, trials, etc.) of this life and inherit an incorruptible crown. Without overcoming sin in this life, there will be no crown. Without the crown there will be no entering the country or city God has prepared for his faithful servants.

Let us look at Abraham and those who died in faith in the scripture text in Hebrews to comprehend how we focus upon a new horizon and not upon the earthly.

In verse eight, when Abraham was called out of his homeland to receive an inheritance, we see, he just did it. He left without any understanding of where he was going or what it would require. Through this call to come out, he was converted from the idolatry of his father's house. He was called out of darkness into God's marvelous light (1 Peter 2:9).

When God calls us out, we, as Abraham, must accept the call and obey. Obeying the call causes us to be born again. We are called out of not only sin, but to separate ourselves from sinful company. It requires us to leave whatever is inconsistent with consecration or total devotion to God.

> 5)*Trust in the Lord with all thine heart; and lean not unto thine own understanding. 6)In all thy ways acknowledge him, and he shall direct thy paths. (Proverbs 3:5 – 6)*

If we trust the Lord, we will not lean unto our own understanding. That means we will not lean to or toward what we think or what we understand. We no longer lean on our perception or how we see things. The Hebrew word is translated as *not to support one's self*. That means we are not to lean on self, not to rely on self, not to rest on self, and not to have confidence in self.

Abraham had no idea of what was ahead for him. He did not try to understand why he was to leave his father's house and go someplace he had never seen. His thoughts were on obedience to God.

Unless we take up our heavy cross of self-denial and do what God's word requires us to do, we will not leave what we are supposed to leave. We will not avoid what we are supposed to avoid. We will never be foreigners in this world. We will have joined the tares growing up with the wheat (Matthew 13:24 – 30). We will no longer stay on the straight and narrow way leading to life but walk on the broad and wide way leading to destruction (Matthew 13:13 – 14).

To follow Christ, we must choose to take up our heavy cross of self-denial. It will, at times, require us to leave worldly connections, to leave worldly comforts, to persevere agony of our flesh, to do something beyond our comprehension.

Although Abraham lived in the promised land, he lived as a sojourner or foreigner ready at all times to move. He knew Canaan was only a type or pledge of a better country, and he kept that better country continually in view. Abraham was always looking to a new horizon.

He kept his focus upon that future city whose builder and maker is God. He always desired that better or heavenly country where God had prepared a city. His affections were not held to this world. He never became so comfortable here that he considered it his home.

Verse fifteen says if he had been mindful of what he left, he would have returned. This reveals if he was held to the temporal, he would have returned to what he left. We see this with the Israelites desiring the fish, leeks, onions, etc. of Egypt (Numbers 11:5).

Their cross of self-denial was too heavy on their flesh and they missed their old life separated from God. However, Abraham did not focus on what he left; his focus was on the new horizon of his eternal abode with God.

> *While we look not at the things which are seen, but at the things which are not seen: for the things which are seen are*

A New Horizon

temporal; but the things which are not seen are eternal. (2 Corinthians 4:18)

Any time we focus on the temporal, and not the eternal, we will find ourselves in what we were delivered from at spiritual birth. Our home is not here. We are not to be content in this world or we have lost focus upon the eternal.

We must never forget we are pilgrims passing through this life looking for a better country. We are looking to a new horizon. Our home is that country where God has prepared a city for us to dwell in for eternity.

How can we have the mindset of looking to a new horizon? We must expect little from this world. We must bear the difficulties of this life with our focus upon our heavenly home. As we seek an incorruptible crown, we will never be content with this world.

When we seek his city, we are not attached to this world no matter how beautiful, how prosperous, etc. We are not attached to anything or anyone in this world. Nothing is worth losing our crown. After all, who or what can we take with us when we die? Everyone and everything is left behind.

How can we know our mind is focused upon a new horizon? Let me ask us some questions revealing where our focus is. Do we speak spiritual things? Does our life portray we are foreigners here? Do we seek the things of God? Do we desire worldly pleasures? Are we doers of the word or hearers only? Does someone or something mean more to us than God? Are we constantly murmuring and complaining? Are we more negative or more positive?

As we consecrate ourselves unto God, we will focus upon a new horizon. We will speak spiritual things. Our life will depict we are foreigners here. We will hunger and thirst for the things of God. We will do his word. No one or nothing will mean more to us than God. We will be content knowing we are in his will.

If we are mindful of what we left, we are focused upon this life. When we place our attention upon what we were delivered from, we will go back. We will return to the idolatrous country where we served false gods of self, people, things, money, fame, etc.

God did not make us leave our bondage, but we chose to do so. Now, once delivered are we missing what we left? Is our life gradually returning to the old country? Are we progressively becoming what we were? Have we become comfortable in the world? Are we focused upon the pleasures of this life?

If we are not taking up our heavy cross of self-denial daily, we will not conquer the impediments trying to cause us to become weary of being foreigners. Instead, we will become at home in this world and take our eyes off a new horizon.

Only as we meditate upon eternal spiritual things, running our race to receive our incorruptible crown will the things of this life have no attraction to us. Such a mindset will cause us to have no desire to return to our old life.

We have set our sight beyond what we see in the natural. We look to a new horizon where God resides. We place no value on this life. Our only God is God Almighty. We worship no one or anything else.

All true believers will desire the better country. The stronger our faith is, the more fervent those desires will be. Our focus will be the new horizon enabling us to persevere, conquer all impediments, receive an incorruptible crown, and reside in a city whose builder and maker is God!

Chapter 11

An Incorruptible Crown

24)Know ye not that they which run in a race run all, but one receiveth the prize? So run, that ye may obtain. 25)And every man that striveth for the mastery is temperate in all things. Now they do it to obtain a corruptible crown; but we an incorruptible. 26)I therefore so run, not as uncertainly; so fight I, not as one that beateth the air: 27)But I keep under my body, and bring it into subjection: lest that by any means, when I have preached to others, I myself should be a castaway. (1 Corinthians 9:24 - 27)

PAUL MAKES CLEAR IF he did not continue to live a disciplined and holy life that takes up his heavy cross of self-denial daily, he could find himself exiled from the Kingdom of God. This is saying he comprehended he could fail altogether to receive an incorruptible crown. This was not a reference to the loss of some reward but to his incorruptible crown. His flesh must be kept under obedience to the word of God which could only be accomplished as he exercised self-control, self-discipline, and self-denial.

God will not take away our salvation. It is the gift of God that is given by faith in Christ's finished work on the cross. Salvation is our birthright and God will not take away His gift. However, we can sell or give away a gift. How many of us have received a gift and sold or gave it away?

We, as Esau, can sell it for a morsel of meat of fornication, adultery, pornography, etc. to satisfy our flesh (Hebrews 12:16). If we continue in that sin until death, we will die in our unrepentant sin. God did not take our salvation, we freely gave it up to satisfy our fleshly appetite.

> *But when the righteous turneth away from his righteousness, and committeth iniquity, and doeth according to all the abominations that the wicked man doeth, shall he live? All his righteousness that he hath done shall not be mentioned: in his trespass that he hath trespassed, and in his sin that he hath sinned, in them shall he die. (Ezekiel 18:24)*

We are utterly deceived by the enemy of the cross if we believe we can never lose our relationship with God. Our sins separate us from Him (Isaiah 59:2). Our salvation is unconditional, but it is not unconditionally secure. There are constant "if" clauses in the word that make this quite clear. We cannot live as we did before and believe we are going to Heaven, if we do despite the Spirit of grace (Hebrews 10:29).

God's soldiers must realize as real soldiers can desert, so can we leave our birthright. Ezekiel makes clear if we die in that condition (unrighteousness), we will die apart from God. Any righteousness done before we turned to unrighteousness will be forgotten. As any unrighteousness done before repenting and turning to righteousness will be forgotten.

> *And grieve not the holy Spirit of God, whereby ye are sealed unto the day of redemption. (Ephesians 4:30)*

When I warned some that our salvation was not unconditionally secure, I was given the verse above. The verse does not claim we are sealed and saved until the day of redemption regardless of any sin in our life.

It does not suggest a seal cannot be tampered with. If we place a seal on something, it can always be broken. The seal implied is the mark He places on us revealing we are his. However, if we grieve to the point of insult to the Spirit of grace, it means total apostasy. We cannot continue in sins of unrighteousness, fornication, idolatry, adultery, homosexuality, extortioners, etc. that will not inherit the Kingdom of God and believe we are going to Heaven (1 Corinthians 6:9 – 10).

The wages of sin is death (Romans 6:23). God's word means what it says. There is no thinking we can live in licentiousness and go to Heaven. The apostle Paul knew this danger. He was aware of the necessity to persevere until he conquered all impediments. He did this by keeping his fleshly appetites in check to avoid the possibility of desertion. He was aware that at any time, we can sell our birthright for the lust of the flesh, the lust of the eyes, and the pride of life. We can experience a right relation with God and then because of our fleshly appetites be carried away from our steadfastness. As Esau, a fleshly appetite will overwhelm us to the point we gladly sell our birthright to satisfy that fleshly desire.

Yes, Jesus will never leave nor forsake us (Hebrews 13:5), but we can leave and forsake Him. That is why Jude wanted believers to guard themselves against false teachers who were preaching dangerous tenets or false doctrines.

How can we be twice dead according to Jude 1:12? When we were born naturally, we were spiritually dead. We were dead in our trespasses and sins and became spiritually alive through the new birth. Then we deserted and died spiritually. We stopped persevering, quit taking up our heavy cross of self-denial, and quit running the race to receive an incorruptible crown.

In Jude 4, he reveals these false teachers had turned the grace of God into lasciviousness which is licentiousness. This is a license for immorality or immoral living. They preached that we could be morally unrestrained or live in sin and go to heaven.

Let me interject how this mentality has many deceived. A woman told me how thankful to God she was for bringing a certain man into her life. I looked at her and asked about her husband. She said he does not understand how the loss of her mother has affected her, whereas so and so is so sympathetic. I told her she was committing adultery and her soul was in danger. She smiled and said, "Once saved, always saved. I am saved and Jesus has forgiven me." I told her the Bible makes clear she is not to be deceived into thinking she will inherit the kingdom of God if she lives as an adulterer (1 Corinthians 6:9).

She came back at me with 1 Corinthians 6:11 and said that her pastor said she is washed, sanctified, and justified by Jesus. I proceeded to tell her the Scripture in 1 Corinthians talks about what she was before she became saved. The verse explicitly states, "such **were** some of you." That means you are no longer guilty of what you have repented of. You have done a 180 degree turn and the sin is now behind you. The verse does not give you license to live immorally and believe you will inherit the kingdom of God. 1 Corinthians 6:9 is clear that no adulterer will go to Heaven.

I told her she is presently an adulterer and unless she repents (no longer lives in adultery), she is going to Hell. In order to be washed, sanctified, and justified, she must no longer live in immorality or disobedience to the Word of God. Christ did not suffer on that cruel cross to give us license to live in the sins He died to deliver us from.

> *Of how much sorer punishment, suppose ye, shall he be thought worthy, who hath trodden under foot the Son of God, and hath counted the blood of the covenant, wherewith he was sanctified, an unholy thing, and hath done despite unto the Spirit of grace? (Hebrews 10:29)*

To deliberately sin after we have received the knowledge of truth is to trample on Jesus. That means that we have no love, respect, etc. for what Christ did for us on the cross. His death was to deliver us from sin, not to allow its deceitfulness to rule in our life. If we do that, we are rejecting his sacrifice for our sins. Rejection means we are refusing the only access that we have to God.

The gospel of lasciviousness creeps in unawares. It overtakes its victim until we are no longer holiness unto the Lord, but a stinking savor of sin. False teachers teach we can be saved and live in sin at the same time. I have even heard some claim our fleshly body has no bearing on our spiritual body. Then why did Jesus live sinless in his fleshly body if the two have no relevance to each other? Plus, we are told in Romans 6:12 that we are **not to let sin reign** in our mortal body that we should obey its lusts. If we allow sin to rule, we will fall victim to its lusts.

Christians are told to study to show themselves approved unto God in order to rightly divide the word of truth (2 Timothy 2:15). Too many want to listen to the teachers of itching ears in order to justify living in the lust of the flesh, the lust of the eyes, and the pride of life. All of which is of the world and not of God (1 John 2:16).

Many start out by faith, persevere for a while, and conquer the impediments hindering our race. But after a while, fleshly appetites try to overcome us. Defection does not happen overnight. It is a process of degeneration as we gradually turn from fighting our flesh to live in holiness and start our decline into lasciviousness or immoral behavior. It begins with a little compromise here and some more compromise there. We start to accept this as not too bad, then we accept that as not too sinful, etc. We start interpreting the word to justify our sin. We are now living as a hearer only and not a doer of God's word.

If we continue to ignore the scriptures and remain in our sinful condition, we will allow our conscience to become seared with a hot iron. When this happens, we no longer sense the prompting of the Holy Spirit and allow the darkness of sin to overcome us. We have permitted our heart to become hardened by sin's deception as Israel did.

That is why Jude exhorts us to earnestly contend for the faith. This means to struggle to the point that our flesh is agonizing from the conflict of following God's directions (his word) or obeying the lust of our flesh. When we quit persevering to conquer impediments meant to destroy our faith, we allow our old man who was crucified with Christ so that we should not serve sin (Romans 6:6) to come back to life in all its carnal appetites. How can we who tasted the goodness of God, once again indulge in sin as a way of life unless our old man has been resurrected? This is not a backslider who feels guilty about sin, will repent (get out of sin), and get right with God.

If our old man is completely back from its crucified state, we no longer yearn for the presence of God. We become comfortable in sin, and feel no guilt, no shame, etc. about sin. We become angry with any who addresses our sinful condition. In short, we have deserted the army of the Lord and are no longer in the race for an incorruptible crown. We have settled for the corruptible crown of this world.

The impediments we must conquer in our life are not meant to discourage us but to teach us obedience to God's word. Jesus became the author of eternal salvation unto all who **obey** him, because He learned through human experience to obey God's word when confronted with severe anguish in his flesh (Hebrews 5:8-9). He took up his heavy cross of self-denial and persevered the cross. Likewise, it is through taking up our heavy cross of self-denial that we learn obedience to God's word which reinforces our faith. Our strengthened faith enables us to persevere, conquer all impediments, and receive an incorruptible crown!

www.ingramcontent.com/pod-product-compliance
Lightning Source LLC
Chambersburg PA
CBHW070321100426
42743CB00011B/2503